SUPERCARS
FIELD GUIDE

Doug Mitchel

Contributing Editor
Tom Collins

©2006 Doug Mitchel
Published by

kp books
An Imprint of F+W Publications

700 East State Street • Iola, WI 54990-0001
715-445-2214 • 888-457-2873

Our toll-free number to place an order or obtain a free catalog is (800) 258-0929.

Library of Congress Catalog Number: 2005906842
ISBN: 0-89689-227-1

Designed by Brian Brogaard
Edited by Tom Collins

Printed in United States of America

Dedication

To my brother Chris:
For achieving all that I have not.

Special Thanks To:

Brumos Porsche, Jacksonville, FL
Continental Auto Sports, Hinsdale, IL
Crossroads Chevrolet, West Chicago, IL
John Gunnell
Fox Valley Motorcars, West Chicago, IL
Dennis Machul
Midtown Imports, Pekin, IL
Ed and Judy Schoenthaler
Supercars.Net
Angelo Van Bogart

Table of Contents

Introduction

In the process of creating this book, I have learned that the word "Supercar" means many things to automotive enthusiasts. Certainly, the Ferrari Enzo is considered by most as perhaps THE Supercar of today, there are many more that exist in the minds of collectors and fans of the genre.

Typically, a "supercar" excels in many arenas, with horsepower at the top of the list. There are vehicles that are based on existing models, but have been enhanced to reach the stratosphere, while others are created solely for that purpose. A few can be purchased by those not related to royalty, or who are in the top 2 percent income bracket, but the majority of the cars seen here are not for the faint of heart or pocketbook.

In addition to the ranks of modern day supercars, I have included a smattering of early examples for comparison. They may not have been tagged with the "supercar" moniker then, but by comparison they met with all the criteria. Their rarity, horsepower and styling set them apart from the more pedestrian offerings, and those that have survived have earned the title today.

BMW North America

| *The champion 1940 BMW MM aerodynamic coupe.*

Introduction

1952 Maserati A6 GCS Series I roadster

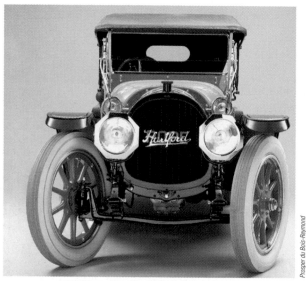

1913 Pope-Hartford Model 29 roadster

Prosper du Bois-Reymond

| *1913 Pope-Hartford Model 29 roadster*

1913 **Pope-Hartford Model 29 roadster**

The 1913 Pope-Hartford was the last of the Pope automotive nova that streaked across the sky in the first decade of the 20th century, the dream of businessman Albert Pope. The Pope-Robinson lasted just two years. The Pope-Toledo was purchased by Overland in 1909. The Pope-Tribune was dead by 1908—purchased, ironically, by the Montrose Metal Casket Company. Pope Manufacturing Co. began in 1876 in Hartford, Connecticut and wheeled into the world of bicycles in 1877. Within 20 years, Pope had consolidated 45 bicycle firms. Seeing the bicycle trend fade, Pope funded an early automobile with the Electric Vehicle Co., the Columbia, in 1897. By 1903, the first Pope-Hartford was tested, a one-cylinder car.

When Colonel Pope died in 1909, his business empire was fading. By 1913, Pope-Hartford was in its third receivership. There were far too many models offered for the meager demand. No more than 700 cars sold in any year they were made. Production figures show just 611 Pope-Hartfords found owners in 1913. Models 31, 33 and 29 were built on a single chassis, each with progressively larger horsepower and wheelbase sizes. The Model 29 was top of the line. The 1913 Pope-Hartford Model 29 roadster had a 133-inch wheelbase and a six-cylinder 60-hp engine.

By 1915, the manufacturing facilities were sold to the Pratt and Whitney empire for $300,000. This is the only Pope-Hartford Model 29 roadster known to exist, a silent witness to an era of brass, wood and steel hands-on craftsmanship.

SUPERCAR STATS	
Engine:	*Overhead valve, long-stroke six*
Displacement:	*471 cid*
Horsepower:	*60 hp*
Bore and stroke:	*4 5/16 x 5 3/8 inches*
Price:	*$4,250*
Note: Only 1913 Pope-Hartford roadster in existence	

1910 Supercars

Prosper du Bois-Reymond

A lot of space produced only modest horses in 1913.

Brass, wood and simplicity marked the dash panel.

Prosper du Bois-Reymond

KP Archives

An early Stutz Bearcat

1914 to 1924 and 1931 to 1933 **Stutz Bearcat**

It was one cat that had two very different lives. In the early days, the Stutz Bearcat was an unrefined racing car. In its second life, it was a French-bodied, gentleman's speedster. Engineer Harry Stutz had worked for American Underslung and the Marmon Motor Car Co. He entered a brand new car at the 1911 Indianapolis 500 and capitalized on its 11th place finish. It sparked the memorable ad slogan "The Car that Made Good in a Day." The Bearcat, which took off after Ideal Car Co. merged with Stutz Auto Parts in 1913, became a sports car icon. By 1915, the Stutz racing team was the chief rival of Mercer's Raceabout. That same year, Cannonball Baker drove a four-cylinder Bearcat from San Diego to New York in just over 11 days.

"It had pistons that resemble ash cans," said venerable automotive writer Tom McCahill in a 1951 retro test. "...[the pistons] drew enough air on the down breath to start a Kansas tornado." The Bearcat became the darling of the young and the flapper crowd beginning in 1915. By 1925, things changed. Stutz had financial problems and new ownership. By 1926, a more conservative era began with the Safety Stutz and Splendid Stutz. In 1932, the new Bearcat, and related Super Bearcat, were brought back to spur sluggish sales but the buyers just weren't there.

Stutz had always advertised that it learned through racing and its early cars, especially the first generation Bearcat, are reminders of and all-out era in American automotive history.

SUPERCAR STATS	
Engine:	4-cylinder, T-head Wisconsin
Displacement:	389.9 cid
Horsepower:	60 hp
0-40:	17.6 seconds
0-60:	29.2 seconds
Top Speed:	80 mph
Weight:	4,500 lbs.
Price:	$2,000

1910 Supercars

KP Archives

1919 Stutz Bearcat

| *1914 to 1927 and 1931 to 1933 Stutz Bearcat*

1920 Stutz Bearcat

KP Archives

KP Archives

1914 Mercer Model 35J Raceabout

1910-1921 **Mercer Raceabout**

In the early days of motoring, the Mercer Raceabout was one of the world's fine cars. As *Automobile Quarterly* recalled in Volume 3, number 4, "Mercer Automobile Company was conceived in the spirit of innovation. Its very first model broke with existing design tradition and adopted the...torpedo style."

In 1911, a Mercer Raceabout with its 300-cid, 34-hp engine won five of six races entered. In 1912, top driver Ralph Da Palma set eight records in his Raceabout and driver Spencer Wishart entered a showroom-new version and won a 200-mile dirt track race. The Raceabout's popularity skyrocketed.

The Raceabout was reliable and light. Drivers could depend on a transmission that shifted smoothly in three (or beginning in 1913, four-speed versions). It had a great power-to-weight combination. The later Raceabouts doubled their power to 70 hp but still were light cars.

"The key to its unflagging appeal lies in its exterior appearance," said writer Mervin Kaufman. "Twin bucket seats, sweeping fender line...and a boldness expressed in a lavish application of brass."

The right-side mounted steering wheel (on early versions) had an unusually long steering column. The hand brake and horn bulb were mounted outside, to the driver's right. Out back were two spare tires. The Mercer Raceabout was always a limited production car. And original prices were above $2,500, heady sticker shock in the day. Original Mercer Raceabouts used a T-head engine with the 70-hp L-head replacing it in 1915.

The Mercers developed a rivalry with the Stutz Bearcat at a race in Corona, California, with Barney Oldfield driving for Mercer. By 1919, the Mercer auto company ran into financial problems that lasted throughout the next decade. The Raceabout has remained in legend long after the company passed away in 1929.

Supercar Classic

1919 Mercer Series Y Raceabout

1914 Mercer Raceabout

Supercar Classic

Doug Mitchel

1927 Bugatti Type 358

1927 **Bugatti Type 35B**

Ettore Bugatti, a prolific automotive designer and innovator, debuted the Type 35 in 1924 for the French Grand Prix. Only trouble with the tires kept it from winning in its first competition. The following year began Bugatti's five-year domination at the Targa Florio event. The 35 would be credited with close to 2,000 victories in the races it entered.

Powered by an inline, 2262cc, eight-cylinder motor, it drew breath through a three-valve cylinder head, and was force-fed by a crankshaft-driven supercharger. A laundry list of options made it a force to be reckoned with. Some 130 horsepower was delivered to the rear drive wheels and the tall and narrow 4.95 x 28-inch tires common to the period. The wheels and brake drums were integrated into a single unit, making for easy inspection of them. The eight-spoke rims were similar to some of today's wheel offerings. Braking remained primitive due to Bugatti's insistence on using cable-operated binders. The 35B was also sold for use as a road-going vehicle for those wealthy and courageous enough to afford the opportunity.

The alloy body was mated to a chassis formed from channel-section steel and held two adults in a rather intimate, side-by-side cockpit. The tapered rear body section spoke volumes about the aerodynamic nature of the beast even when it was at rest. The only protection from the elements came from a tiny windscreen on the driver's side. The turned-metal dash added a touch of beauty to the otherwise austere interior.

The Type 35 remains one of the most desired Bugattis of all time with values determined by the buyer's bank account and the seller's willingness to part with a truly scarce machine.

SUPERCAR STATS	
Displacement:	2262cc (138 cid)
Engine Layout:	Inline eight
Horsepower:	130@5200rpm
Top Speed:	125 mph
Transmission:	Four-speed manual

Doug Mitchel

1927 Bugatti Type 358

| *1927 Bugatti Type 35B*

Doug Mitchell

The engine of the 1927 Bugatti Type 358.

Doug Mitchel

The Bentley 4-1/2 liter in a racing environment.

1928 **Bentley 4-1/2 liter**

With the railroads his first passion, and source of enormous wealth, Walter Owen Bentley had a desire to incorporate some of the same engineering traits that were being used on locomotives of the day. His machines were never small, but were powerful and had terrific handling.

Among the most famous machines created by Bentley were the 4-1/2 liter cars destined for success at the 24 Hours of Le Mans. His first attempt was made in a prototype 1927 variation, but a major crash ended his dreams for that event. Proving his design worthy, a 4-1/2 liter Bentley won the 1928 endurance race with no water left in the engine block. His intent to build heavy, dependable machines had been established with this victory. Neither the 1928 or 1929 cars were supercharged, yet they continued their winning ways. W.O. Bentley was not a fan of motors driven by superchargers, but a driver installed an Amherst Villiers unit in a 1930 4-1/2 and records began to fall. These supercharged models are some of the rarest and most desirable machines today.

The 4-1/2 liter motor was of an inline-four nature, with four valves per pot. A single overhead cam stirred the valves to life and an extended stroke was measured upon inspection. Being of cast-iron construction, weight savings was not an issue. While its ladder frame was massive, its coachwork was a mixture of steel and fabric, saving a few scant ounces in the process. The lack of a driver's door simply aided in access during a race, but did little for safety issues. A quartet of enormous drum brakes hauled the 4,200-pound machine to rest.

SUPERCAR STATS	
Engine:	Inline-four, supercharged
Displacement:	4-1/2 liters (274 cid)
Engine Layout:	Front-mounted
Horsepower:	110 hp with supercharger
Top Speed:	124 mph
Weight:	4,200 lbs.

Doug Mitchel

The 4-1/2 liter engine gave this Bentley its name.

KP ARchives

A British flag seems fitting on this Bentley 4-1/2 liter.

1928 Bentley 4-1/2 liter | 29

Prosper du Bois-Reymond

The Bentley engine propelled the car to racing victories.

1929 and 1930 **"Blower" Bentley**

Secret agent James Bond drove one in the original Ian Fleming novels. Television viewers got used to seeing one in the late 1960s thanks to John Steed in the "Avengers."

The 1929 and 1930 "Blower" Bentley was named for its protruding supercharger that boosted the power available to the 4.5 liter engine. The "blower" was a Roots supercharger that brought horsepower from the 120 range to an amazing 242. More than 148 inches long, the Bentley weighed over two tons, one of the heaviest cars to ever circle a Grand Prix track. Yet years later, a reviewer found the car was even-tempered, smooth and impressed everyone who saw it on its test run.

Walter Owen (W.O.) Bentley enjoyed competition but wasn't sold on the blower. He thought it would "...pervert its design and corrupt its performance." The "Blower" Bentley was developed to win the 24 Hours of Le Mans and cost $2,000 more than the standard version. Some 54 production versions were eventually made by the Bentley works at Cricklewood.

The "Bentley Boys" racing team of Woolf Barnato, Sir Henry Birkin, George Duller, Glen Kidston, Sammy Davis and Dr. Dudley Benjafield were successful. Birkin later modified the 4.5 liter Bentley and raced against the Bentley "Speed Sixes" at Le Mans in 1930.

For Bentley, who built airplane engines for the Sopworth Camel of World War I, the "Blower Bentley" became a legend and a supercar in the process.

Prosper du Bois-Reymond

The exposed supercharger gave this Bentley its name.

The Bentley was powerful but not a petite car.

KP Archives

1932 Duesenberg J Derham-bodied tourer

1929 to 1935 **Duesenberg J**

The Duesenberg might fit the all-time definition of "world-class supercar." The Duesenberg J became the platform for some of the most beautiful coachwork in automobile history and was the perfect car in terms of its engine and chassis to adapt to many designs.

Perhaps no other car in American automotive history has been as "super" as the Duesenberg J as crafted by Fred and Augie Duesenberg.

By 1929, the Duesenberg car company was working its way out of financial problems thanks to the influx of financing of E. L. Cord, who also was working with the Auburn and Cord companies.

The Duesenberg brothers were given carte blanche to build the best car possible. Many automotive enthusiasts today would agree they accomplished their goal.

With a standard straight-eight that produced 265 hp, the Duesenberg had plenty of power to fit any occasion and to carry creative coachwork in both 142.5-inch or 153.5-inch varieties.

The Gordon Buehrig-designed Duesenbergs had some body choices crafted in-house but many more were finished by the best of the world's coachwork shops. Duesenberg J cars were customized by Bonham and Schwartz, Le Baron, La Grande, Derham, Holbrook, Judkins, Rollston, Weymann and Willoughby, to name a few.

The Duesenberg J's production ended in 1935 but several chassis continued to be worked on in 1936 and 1937. Sadly, no new Duesenbergs would follow. The Duesenbergs became collectible vehicles even in Depression Era North America and today are some of the most desired vehicles in the world. A 1931 Duesenberg J Le Baron convertible sedan sold for $440,000 in a recent auction.

1920 Supercars

Blackhawk Collection

1931 Duesenberg J Murphy-bodied roadster

1932 Duesenberg J Derham-bodied tourer

KP Archives

1928 Stutz Black Hawk roadster

1929 **Stutz Vertical Eight Model M & Stutz Black Hawk**

While the name is lost to the generations born after World War II, "The Car That Made Good in a Day" was comparable to Cadillac, Packard and Duesenberg as a world-class supercar.

Harry Stutz designed his own racing cars beginning in 1911. The Stutz cars were sturdy and reliable. Soon, Stutz was producing cars like the Bulldog and Bearcat that were tough, fast and very sporty. The Stutz Bearcat roadsters became a 1920s icon.

Financial problems plagued Stutz and by 1925, new leader Frederick Moskovics planned to turn the "hairy" Stutz into a more stately car. The "Safety Stutz" and "Splendid Stutz" were new directions. By 1928, Stutz showed its refined Black Hawk Speedster, a boat-tailed production version of the famed 1927 Stutz Black Hawk racer that won every AAA stock car race it entered. French bodymaker Charles Weymann began a working relationship with Stutz.

The 1929 Stutz Vertical Eight Model M coupe exemplified the refined Stutz with dual sidemount tires, a trunk, leather interior and extra chrome. The Stutz had power with its 322-cid, 115 hp straight-eight and four-speed transmission. In 1931, the DV 32 Stutz (referring to its number of valves) provided a platform for fine body builders. The Bobcat and Super Bobcat revived the glory of the classic Bearcats before production ended in 1935. Stutz had always used racing as the true test of its products. "Judge the Stutz by the standard of actual performance and a coninuous trustworthiness," said a Stutz ad in the 1920s. Today, many recognize Stutz as a great name in supercar history.

SUPERCAR STATS	
Engine:	*SOHC straight-eight*
Displacement:	*322 cid*
Engine Layout:	*Front-mounted*
Horsepower:	*115 hp*
Pride:	*$3,595 (with options)*

Note: One of four 1929 Stutz M coupes remaining.

Angelo Van Bogart

1929 Stutz Vertical 8 "M"

Angelo Van Bogart

All Stutz cars were advertised as race-tested.

1907 Fiat 130

Prosper du Bois-Reymond

Supercars and the Racing Heritage

From the very beginning of automaking, racing cars in various forms of competition—rallies, hill climbs, dirt track, frozen ponds, circular tracks, cross-country and cross-continental challenges—all helped sort out the hype from the reality of auto performance.

In Europe and North America, competition enhanced reputations. Pioneers like Henry Ford knew competition proved durability and invigorated the bottom line. Many early automakers believed that word of mouth and "seeing is believing" were key elements in promoting their cars. Many cars succeeded in building reputations in competitions.

One of the early competitors was the 1907 Fiat 130-hp racer. The French had dominated early 1900s racing and Fiat of Italy was determined to stem that tide. Designer Giovanni Enrico designed a smooth, chain-driven two-seater with a 16,286cc (or a whopping 993 cid!) engine. The Fiat behemoth power plant weighed 2,000 lbs.

Long before Chrysler, the Fiat used hemispherical combustion chambers, a design Bugatti would also use successfully in years to come. The Fiat proudly won the Sicilian-based Targa Florio as well as the French Grand Prix and a German race.

Racing didn't save everyone. The legendary Marmon Wasp, the Peerless Green Dragon, and Thomas Flyer are just a few examples of race cars that outlasted parent companies.

Competition success stories have often produced supercar status and often have been a litmus test for a automaker success stories.

SUPERCAR STATS	
Engine:	Fiat four-cylinder
Displacement:	16,286cc (993 cid)
Engine Layout:	Front-mounted
Horsepower:	130 hp
Weight:	The engine alone weighed 2,000 lbs.

Note: The car was chain-driven.

Prosper du Bois-Reymond

This closeup shows the chain drive on the Fiat 130.

1917 Peerless "Green Dragon"

KP Archives

1930s Bugatti Type 55 roadster

Ettore Bugatti's Cars for the Pure Breds

In 1909, Ettore Bugatti gave himself a Christmas present, an auto production company in the Alsace region of France at Molsheim, near Strasbourg.

"Le Patron" Bugatti was multi-dimensional man, a one-of-a-kind person who did everything with style and elan and his cars were the same way. He would build everything from a miniature of a famed racing car to a self-powered railroad car in his career.

When someone complained about a malfunction in a Bugatti, journeying three times from Paris to the factory to explain the problem, Bugatti simply told the owner to stop. In Bugatti's mind there was no problem. When a European monarch wanted to buy a Type 41 La Royale Bugatti, he was refused after Bugatti observed the royal's "abhorrent" table manners.

The best way to describe the car's reputation was written in the Apr. 14, 1921 Automotive Journal:

"...I regard the Bugatti as a car of a thousand...there is nothing like it. England, France, Italy, or America have nothing to offer which can match it."

A long list of Bugattis have become famous—and precious—as supercars. One of the all-time great racers is the 1924 Type 35 Bugatti. Many like the rakish Atlantic and Atalante coupes. TheBugatts called themselves the "Pur Sang des Automobiles" which can be translated as the prebred automobile. A gear clicked as one Bugatti series gained speed, annoying drivers. "That's the way it should be," said Le Patron, firm in what he had made.

SUPERCAR STATS	
Engine:	W-16, Quad-OHC
Displacement:	8.0 liters (488 cid)
Engine Layout:	Mid-mounted
Horsepower:	736 hp
0 to 100:	2.9 seconds
Top Speed:	248 mph (limited)
Weight:	4,300 lbs.
Price:	$1.3 million

Supercar Classic

KP Archives

1932 Bugatti Type 50 coupe

1930s Bugatti Drophead

1926 Lincoln Judson-bodied limousine

1930s **Lincoln K Series**

The so-called "Master of Precision," Henry M. Leland, gave the world two supercars through his work—the Cadillac and the Lincoln. Leland sold his Lincoln interests to Ford Motor Co. in 1922 offering Ford a top-shelf model.

In 1931, a new K series design would propel Lincoln to a new level of popularity. The K-series Lincolns were 145 inches long, had a frame that was nine inches deep and was lower and sleeker. It also was more powerful with a 120-hp V-8—later upgraded to 125 horsepower. And for the final power coup de gras, a 448-cid, 150-hp V-12 was added to the mix.

Following on the well-mannered heels of the K series was the KB Lincoln. Coachmakers found it the perfect car for their bodymaking efforts. Custom bodies by Brunn, Dietrich, Judkins, Le Baron and Murphy all became true classics that still are admired.

In 1934, Lincoln morphed the K and KB versions into a new KV series while also maintaining the K and KB cars. That gave the bodymakers even greater opportunities.

The 1930s also brought two more styling advances from Lincoln. One was the John Tjaarda-based Lincoln-Zephyr with its sleek and futuristic unit body. The second was an offshoot of the Zephyr design. Edsel Ford asked to have a one-off Lincoln-Zephyr built for his use. The design influenced what would become the Lincoln Continental.

All Lincolns seem to draw from the roots of precision set forth by Henry Leland as well as the high standards of the K, KB and KV Lincolns of the 1930s. They are supercars that everyone, especially enthusiasts of the Ford-Lincoln-Mercury persuasion, can be proud of owning and admiring.

KP Archives

1934 Lincoln KB V-12 sedan

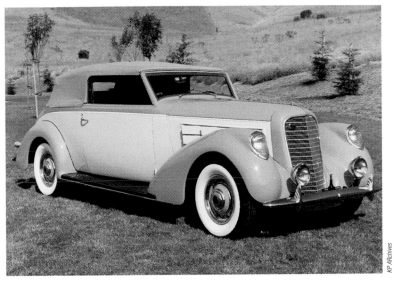

1937 Lincoln K Brunn-Bodied Convertible Victoria

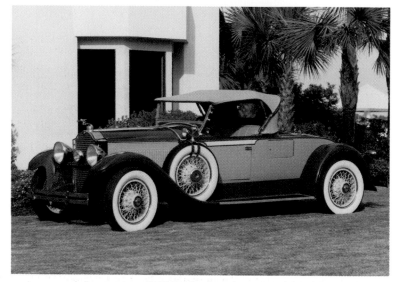

1929 Packard roadster

Classic 1930s Packards

Prestige carmaker Packard took a long slide from prominence to its demise in 1958. Yet, from 1899 and for more than 55 years or more, the Packard's place was in the ranks of the top world super cars, especially in the first half of the 20th century.

Early Packards were well-built, durable cars in both four and six-cylinder versions. Already in their earliest days, the Packards were receiving elaborate, personalized bodywork. That would continue and the Packard's prestige would grow with the Twin Six and various eight-cylinder models.

The "Goddess of Speed" reigned over tremendous styling achievements by coachmakers who used the Packard chassis to produce works of art by Brunn, Dietrich, Le Baron, Rollston and others are probably the best remembered Packards of the 1930s and early 1940s.

Packard Senior Eights and Twelves were natural vehicles for the personalization and customization that coachwork embodied. Refined, quiet and elegant, these Packards turned heads constantly in Depression Era America.

And Packard's tradition of listing their model years in terms of epochs only added to the allure. The Tenth Series or the Sixteenth Series sounded so elegant and stylish.

Packards also maintained styling cues like the slanted yet strongly vertical radiator on its prow. Picking 1937, the Fifteenth Series, as a typical year for Packards, they were available in 134-, 139- and 144-inch wheelbases among the various body styles. More than 25 styles were available including a formal sedan, a business limousine, a Le Baron-bodied cabriolet, a convertible sedan, a victoria and more.

"Ask the man who owns one" was the longtime slogan and many men—and women—longed to own a Packard. Others still admire these classic, well-built cars. They are quiet, dignified and timelessly elegant.

KP Archives

1929 Packard Dietrich-bodied dual cowl phaeton

1933 Packard Twelve dual cowl phaeton

KP Archives

1924 Hispano-Suiza H6B 32cv Torpedo by Jean-Henri Labourdette Carrosserie, Paris

Hispano-Suizas

The venerable Hispano-Suiza is a member of supercar royalty. It was literally a car chosen by a king, Alfonso XIII of Spain in 1905. And Hispano-Suiza returned the favor beginning in 1909 with the Alfonso XIII model.

The truly regal Hispano-Suizas taken together are works of art and, like great works of art, their rarity, design and prestige only drives up their value with time.

All the great automotive coachwork masters worked on the "Hisso" canvas including the French Henri Binder, Bevalette, Chapron, Duvivier, Letourner et Marchand, Vanden Plas and Weymann as well as lesser known Spanish body works like Norte of Oviedo and Pareja of Granada. Some of the most memorable Hispano-Suizas of the 1920s were crafted by Labourdette and Ortega of Madrid. The first Cadillac offspring La Salles were inspired by these designs.

Some Hispano-Suiza owners preferred seasonal motoring. That is, they chose one body for their car's chassis for the summer and another for winter, like suits of clothing.

The fine car company also made buses, trucks, various engines and airplane-related items. World War I airplane engines brought fame to Hispano-Suiza in several ways. Designer Mark Berkigt, a Swiss-born engineer/ designer, won the French Legion of Honor for his work with a French airplane. Aero engineering found its way into the 1919 H6 series. Also, *la cocogne volante,* the flying stork that became the H-S logo, came from a French aero squadron

One famous "Hissos" of the 1920s was built by aircraft maker Nieuport in 1924. It used an 8.0 liter (488 cid) engine and was raced at Targa Florio in Italy.

While the stork has always been considered good luck in Europe, the Great Depression of the 1930s meant declining business. The company, with plants in Spain, France, and Switzerland, remained in business but its car production ended in 1937.

1935 Hispano-Suiza Chapron limousine

Hispano-Suiza town sedan

KP Archives

1931 Bugatti Royale Type 41 Binder-bodied coupe de ville

1931 Bugatti Royale (Type 41)

Only six of raconteur/carmaker Ettore Bugatti's dream cars, the huge Bugatti Royale, were made and only three of them were sold. Two are considered official treasures of France, on a par with the Eiffel Tower.

Chassis 41 100: This original prototype had four bodies in its lifetime—a Packard, a Bugatti sedan, a Weymann and the Jean Bugatti-designed coupe' Napoleon. It was Ettore Bugatti's personal car until he died in 1947.

Chassis 41 111: The first Royale sold went to textile magnate Armand Esders with an Henri Binder roadster body. Later, Jean Bugatti designed the coupe' chauffeur body for it.

Chassis 41 121: Purchased by Dr. Josef Fuchs of Munich, Germany, it received a Ludwig Weinberger body and cost $43,000 in 1932. Its world odyssey ended in 1943 when it was nearly scrapped in New York City. Saved by a GM executive, it belongs to the Henry Ford Museum.

Chassis 41 131: This last Royale sold went to C. W. Foster of England who ordered a limousine body from Park Ward. In 1956, the car sold to an American collector for $8,000.

Chassis 41 141: Bugatti commissioned Kellner to make a sleek Royale coach for the 1932 London Olympia Show. At $32,500, it was the most expensive car displayed. L'Ebe'Bugatti sold the car to the Briggs Cunningham Museum.

Chassis 41 150: The second Cunningham purchase from Mdme. Bugatti was the double berline de voyage, covered with wood veneer. Later in the Nethercutt Collection, Bill Harrah purchased it in 1964 for $45,000.

Left with 23 Type 41 engines, Bugatti designed a railroad locomotive, the autorail, that used two or four of them for power, the "Pure Bred of the Rails." In a letter to his son, Jean, the elder Bugatti commented that perfection is never reached. Yet the Royale must rank close to supercar perfection.

KP Archives

A profile view of the 1931 Bugatti Royale Type 41 Kellner coach.

KP Archives

Here is the 1931 Bugatti Royale Weymann-bodied formal sedan.

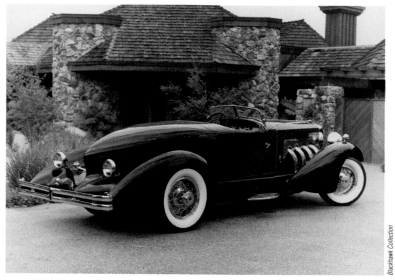

Blackhawk Collection

1931 Duesenberg SJ Figoni and Falaschi-bodied "French Speedster"

1932-1935 **Duesenberg SJ**

After shaking out of its financial problems, Duesenberg Inc. was a reformed company in 1926 and this time the owner was Erret Loban Cord, who told Fred Duesenberg to build a world-class car. On December 1, 1928, the J series Duesenberg premiered at the New York Automotive Salon.

With both 142.5 and 153.5-inch wheelbase sizes, the Duesenberg was longer than many cars of its era and even at 5,000 pounds or more, depending on the body style, it became one of the world's most famous supercars.

Many Duesenberg SJs were coach-built vehicles but the company also sold some of its own body styles designed by Gordon Buehrig.

One might call the SJ version of the grand Duesenbergs the last testimony to the greatness of Fred Duesenberg. Not long after he'd designed the supercharged version, he died in a car accident in 1932. He designed the centrifugal supercharger that boosted the J's horsepower output to 320. Later, Augie Duesenberg's touch made the engine produce an even 400 horsepower.

In 1935, driver Ab Jenkins took a Duesenberg SJ to 152.1 mph on the Bonneville Salt Flats and he averaged 135.5 mph over 24 hours in an SJ Special.

The Duesenberg's production lifetime was in an era when most cars, if people could afford them at all, were priced in hundreds of dollars. The mighty Duesenberg J and SJ were out of the range of most people in North America.

The Duesenberg J and SJ as well as JN and SSJ versions, became incredible icons of the American and world automotive worlds. Even when they were new, these supercharged cars were the supercars that people admired and Duesenbergs have never ceased to be members of the supercar class of fine autos.

1930 Supercars

KP Archives

This 1935 SSJ was actor Clark Gable's Duesenberg.

KP Archives

A 1937 Bonham and Schwartz-bodied Duesenberg SJ.

Doug Mitchel

1933 Alfa-Romeo 8C Monza

1933 Alfa-Romeo 8C Monza

Introduced in a time when the world economy was in turmoil, Alfa-Romeo stubbornly rolled out the new 8C 2300 to great acclaim. Sold as a "street" car, it was also raced in almost every major event available. Both cars entered in the first Mille Miglia were destroyed in collisions, but subsequent Monzas racked up many wins. With the likes of Tazio Nuvolari behind the wheel, winning was a foregone conclusion.

Using the popular inline, eight-cylinder motor of the period, the 8C made good use of the design. Displacing 2,336cc, and running with two-valve heads, the Alfa mill produced 142 hp and reached a top speed of 106 mph.

To achieve these numbers, a Roots-type supercharger was also in place to boost output. A single carburetor processed the pressurized air and fuel mixture. That was the civilian version's performance. The car pictured here was the Monza, the racing version of the car.

The Monza iteration rode on the short wheelbase, and was often stripped of its pontoon fenders for use in racing. This example still sports the sheet metal fenders and is used on suburban streets.

Some were made in single-seat versions but most carried the two-person layout. In The Monza's era a co-driver was common in racing.

The road-going 8C was seen with a full-width windscreen and provided a minimalist convertible top for use in inclement weather.

The Monza was devoid of these frivolous items in an attempt to get down to fighting trim.

SUPERCAR STATS	
Transmission:	*Four-speed manual*
Displacement:	*2336cc (142.5 cid)*
Engine Layout:	*Inline eight*
Horsepower:	*142@5200 rpm*
Top Speed:	*106 mph*

1930 Supercars

Doug Mitchel

The 8C Monza brought racing glory to Alfa-Romeo.

A trophy-winning 1938 Alfa-Romeo 8C 2900B.

Prosper du Bois-Reymond

The beautiful lines of the Van Vooren-bodied Hispano-Suiza.

1933 Hispano-Suiza J-12 (Type 68) Van Vooren Faux Cabriolet

Hispano-Suizas were famous for their performance and quality. One improvement sought in the late 1920s was noise reduction, although a minor problem compared to some cars. Hispano-Suiza engineer/designer Mark Berkigt created a new engine, based on airplane technology that solved the problem. Its seven-main bearing crank weighed 70 lbs. but was machined from a 970 block of metal. The camshaft had 24 lobes for maximum power and silence.

The Type 68 premiered at the 1931 Paris Auto Salon. Only the Maybach Zeppelin compared with the 200-hp (488-cid) V-12. Just 120 of the Type 68s were built at the Bois-Colombes, France, factory from September 1931 through November 1938. The cars came in four chassis lengths: 15 feet (Short); 16 feet (Light); 16 feet, 3 inches (Normal); and 16 feet, 11 inches (Long). Wheelbases were 11 feet, 2 inches on the Light and Normal and 13 feet, 2 inches on the Long.

A contemporary road test reported: "The set of figures obtained from this car are one of an amazing order, surpassing...any similar set of test data recorded by *The Autocar*."

The Type 68 (J 12) pictured is chassis 14501 with engine 321049. Formerly owned by bodymaker Charles Weyman, it is a faux cabriolet, a coach with a cabriolet-style roof, made by Van Vooren.

The Type 68 is a testament to Berkigt and to everyone associated with Hispano-Suiza.

SUPERCAR STATS	
Engine:	Hispano-Suiza Type 68 V-12
Displacement:	9.0 liters (549.2 cid)
	Optional : 11.3 liter (689 cid)
Engine Layout:	Front-mounted
Horsepower:	190 hp (9.0 liter)
	220 hp (11.3 liter)
Top Speed:	100 mph
0 to 50:	9.25 seconds
0 to 60:	12 seconds

Prosper du Bois-Reymond

1933 Hispano-Suiza Type 68 (J12) Van Vooren Faux Cabriolet

The stork was the symbol of luck for the Hispano-Suiza.

KP Archives

1933 Morgan Super Sports three-wheeler

1933 Morgan Super Sports (Three-Wheeler)

In an era when cars could be large and rather cumbersome, Henry Frederick Stanley Morgan, a former engineer at the Swindon Works in England, tried something different. He had opened the Malvern Link garage, a Wolseley and Darracq dealership, in 1906. Looking for something new to drive, he took a Peugeot 7-hp engine and began working.

"I never cared for motorcycles," he recalled in a first-person magazine article. "I therefore decided to fit the engine into a light, three-wheeled chassis I designed."

College professor Stephenson Peach helped Morgan prepare two three-wheelers for the Olympia Motor Show in 1911. Morgan decided to "make a few," as he described it and his father, Rev. Prebendary H.G. Morgan, invested in the venture. Simplicity and durability made the Morgan three-wheelers popular. In the Super Sports, as in many Morgan three-wheelers, the engine was out front and uncovered. The Super Sports was a so-called "barrelback" Morgan and was produced from 1927 through 1939. By 1933, the Morgan was powered by the Matchless 990cc engine.

"...our success lies in the fact that we offer the public a simple and sound machine of light weight and good performance," said Morgan.

He forgot to mention fun! Morgan, who raced in rallies always accompanied by his wife, must have enjoyed driving.

And fun certainly is one definition of a supercar—whether it's the 1933 Morgan Super Sports or any of the other great Morgan cars.

SUPERCAR STATS	
Engine:	Matchless (Also Matchless MX2 (air cooled) and MX4 (water cooled)
Displacement:	990cc
Engine Layout:	Front-mounted, uncovered
Horsepower:	42 hp
Compression:	6.2 : 1

1930 Supercars

Patrick Paternie

The 1934 Family was a Morgan Super Sports variation.

The Morgan three-wheeler was a versatile vehicle.

Prosper du Bois-Reymond

1933 Napier-Railton

1933 **Napier-Railton**

In 1933, when people attempted to set a new speed record or to win a race, they considered the bigger the better. In the case of the Napier-Railton, they were thinking in truck like terms! John Rhodes Cobb, called the "Gentle Giant," liked big cars. With wealth he acquired in the fur trade, Cobb went into racing at the Brooklands Race Track in England. In 1926, he drove a 10-liter (610-cid) 1911 Fiat to victory. He bought a pair of 10.5-liter (640-cid) Delages and raced them at Brooklands from 1929 to 1933.

The Napier-Railton was a Cobb-sized supercar! It used a 24 liter (a whopping 1,463 cid) 12 cylinder Napier Lion airplane engine that developed 500 hp. The car set a Brooklands track record at 143.44 mph on Oct. 7, 1935.

It broke the World Record for 24 Hours, then a competition, with 137.4 mph in 1935 and upped that mark to 150.6 mph in 1936. The big bruiser cruised to a new world record at the Bonneville Salt Flats in Utah at 152.7 mph the same year.

Cobb went on to build the Mobil Railton with twin Napier engines. He set a new Bonneville record of 394.19 mph that same year and was the first person to surpass 400 mph. In 1952, Cobb lost his life trying to set a speed record on water.

Prosper du Bois-Reymond

This was one car made for people who liked full-sizes.

Today, the Napier-Railton is well preserved displayed and is on display at the Brooklands Race Track Museum.

Only a few people are allowed to drive it these days—among them "Mr. Bean" and the "Black Adder," actor Rowan Atkinson!

SUPERCAR STATS	
Engine:	12-cylinder Napier Lion aero engine
Displacement:	24 liters (1,284 cid)
Engine Layout:	Front-mounted
Horsepower:	500 hp
Top Speed:	157.44 mph, 1936 Bonneville Salt Flats record

KP Archives

1935 Mercedes-Benz 500K convertible "Spezial roadster"

1934 **Mercedes-Benz 500K**

One of the many memorable Mercedes-Benz supercars came in 1934 with the 500K. It replaced the two-ton 380 series that was considered to be underpowered with a 3.8-liter, 120 hp engine. Mercedes wanted a new car to rival the Adler and Horch on the new autobahns. The 500K used a 5.0-liter, 160 hp straight-eight engine.

An *Autocar* test referred to buyers getting two Mercedes for the $5,000 price tag: "At 60 unblown there hardly appears to be movement. 70 is an amble and even 80 scarcely noticed." The story continued that a second, almost demonic car howled to life when the supercharger was kicked on and its gauges "...leap around their dials."

Said a British driver: "[The 500K] is one of the few cars to raise envy in the hearts of real motorists." One observer said its 3,000 lbs. was a good attribute because a lighter car would be too dangerous to drive. A 16.5 second 0 to 60 time and more than 100 mph top speed must have made the team of Hans Nibel and Dr. Ferdinand Porsche proud of the new creation.

Styled by Hermann Ahrens, the 500K used independent rear suspension with swing arms and was stopped with Bosch-Dewandre vacuum-boosted hydraulic brakes.

In an era when "super" took on some bizarre connotations in German politics and society, the 500K really was superlative. And it got even better when the 540K was introduced with even more horsepower.

SUPERCAR STATS	
Engine:	5.0 liter (306.3 cid), ohv, supercharged
Bore & Stroke:	3.39 x 4.25 inches
Engine Layout:	Front-mounted inline-8
Horsepower:	160 hp
Top Speed:	100+ mph
0 to 60::	16 seconds
Price:	$10,780

1930 Supercars

KP Archives

1936 Mercedes-Benz 540K 3-position Windovers convertible

More horsepower came with the 540K version.

1936 BMW 328

Prosper du Bois-Reymond

1936-1940 BMW 328 and 328MM

As the world was sliding toward the brink of war, the Bavarian Motor Worken (BMW) was producing several cars including a lightweight sports car that became a legend.

The stylish 328 roadster's front carried the twin narrow radiator grilles that became a BMW symbol and still are used today. The 328's lines flowed to its rounded back that lacked bumpers but carried a spare tire inset in the deck lid. Its cut-down, rear-hinged doors opened to a practical interior with a large steering wheel and round gauges. With fender skirts attached in back, the 328 and Jaguar XK-120 that came a decade later bore a striking resemblance.

The 328 used a 1,971cc (120.3 cid) inline-six that produced 80.1 horsepower and was coupled to a four-speed transmission. The 328 cars would rule 2.0 liter racing between 1937 and 1940 with their engines using three carburetors and producing 80 to 100 more horsepower than the standard 325 engine. The basic 328 engine had two overhead valves per cylinder and produced 93 lbs.-ft. of torque at 4,000 rpm. The standard 328 weighed just 1,830 lbs.

Six Mille Miglia roadsters were built for competition between 1937 and 1940. They had a strengthened chassis, improved tuning and added horsepower. The 1939 aerodynamic 328 MM coupe and 1940 aluminum superleggera versions were built for competition.

The little BMW 328 roadster earned its reputation as a supercar.

SUPERCAR STATS	
Engine:	Overhead valve, inline-six
Displacement:	1971cc (120.3 cid)
Engine Layout:	Front-mounted
Horsepower:	80.1 hp (135 hp and more, racing versions)
Top Speed:	120 mph
Torque:	93 lbs.-ft. @ 4,000 rpm
Weight:	1,830 lbs.

1930 Supercars

The BMW 328 was a popular roadster.

Prosper du Bois-Reymond

BMW's 328 was a pre-World War II success.

1930 Supercars

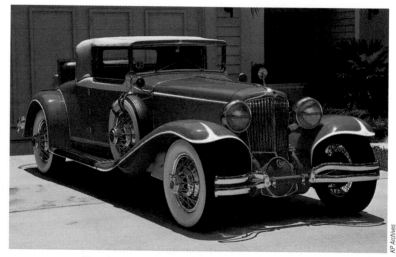

KP Archives

The classic look of the 1930 Cord L-29 cabriolet.

1936 and '37 **Cord 810 and 812**

Erret Loban Cord was no shrinking violet. He went from selling used cars in Los Angeles in 1920 to the chief stockholder of the Auburn car company later in the decade. Soon he would own Auburn, Checker, Duesenberg, Lycoming engine and several other companies.

He revitalized Auburn literally with flashy paint and fast salesmanship. He brought in the Duesenberg brothers and their tremendous car line. Cord even named a car for himself. But by 1932, the Depression had put the Cord automotive empire on the ropes.

In his own style, Cord created excitement from chaos promoting rumors of a "baby Duesenberg" and new 12- and 16-cylinder engines. A deal with Montgomery-Ward breathed $500,000 worth of life into the scattered new car project that became the 1936 Cord. Designer Gordon Buehrig recalled the cars were rushed into production.

The cars that would be designed and produced on something of a shoestring in automotive industry terms would become a legendary automobile.

The 810 and 812 Cords featured front-wheel drive with a 288.6 cid Lycoming V-8. Styling included a "coffin-nosed" hood, pontoon fenders and minimal chrome on a sleek body. The supercharged versions got to 60 mph in just 13 seconds, one of the fastest cars of the era.

Westchester and Beverly sedans, a Sportsman two-passenger coupe and a four-passenger convertible Cord called the Phaeton were 1936 models. A custom Beverly and Custom Berline were added in 1937.

Cords used an electrically-assisted pre-select four-speed transaxle, an innovation prone to problems. While the new Cord's U-joints were better than the earlier L-29 car, they reportedly developed a great deal of noise. The 1936 and '37 Cords rank among the supercars and seem new almost 70 years later. E. L. Cord sold his automotive interests but continued promoting, making his fortune again in real estate and later entering politics.

1930 Supercars

KP Archives

A brightly painted Cord 812 Phaeton in the sun.

1936 Cord 812 Phaeton

1930 Supercars

Doug Mitchel

1939 Cadillac V-16 Opera Coupe

1939 Cadillac V-16 Opera Coupe

The earliest days of the Cadillac brand were in 1902. As time passed it would become revered and respected as one of America's premier builders of fine automobiles. Some of the world's most opulent automobiles were built in the 1920s and '30s, with names like Duesenberg, Packard and Hispano-Suiza selling cars alongside Cadillac. The competition led to engine cylinders and displacements that grew into new categories.

1930 saw the use of a V-16 motor in the Cadillac line, and the smoothness and power was among the best in the world. Cadillac introduced their latest "second series" V-16 in 1938, and those engines made their way into 1,039 models. The new editions ran with 431-cubic inch displacement versus the 452 seen in the earlier Caddy V-16.

Although it was smaller in displacement, the engine was still rated at 185 horsepower. Square bore and stroke dimensions of 3.25 inches for each cylinder were responsible for the engine's smoothness. Improvements to the Cadillac V-8 made them almost as smooth as the big V-16, and sales lagged accordingly. 1940 would be the final year of application for the V-16 engine was used in a Cadillac. The V-16 was only offered to those buying the Series 90 cars.

One of them was the Opera Coupe seen here. A lengthy 141.3-inch wheelbase carried the stylish two-door body, with its covered fender-mounted sidemounts and tasteful dashes of chrome. This Cadillac proudly lived up to the marque's "Standard of Excellence."

SUPERCAR STATS	
Engine:	V-16
Displacement:	288.6 cid
Engine Layout:	Front mounted
Horsepower:	185 hp
Wheelbase:	141.3 inches (Series 90)
Years of Prod.:	Second Series V-16, 1938 to 1940

The 1939 Cadillac V-16 Opera Coupe was an impressive car.

A 1938 Cadillac V-16 convertible.

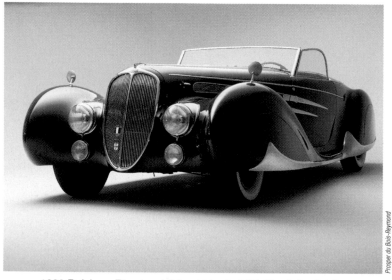

Prosper du Bois-Reymond

1939 Delahaye Figoni and Falaschi-bodied "California" cabriolet

| *1939 Delahaye "California" Figoni et Falaschi Cabriolet*

1939 Delahaye "California" Figoni et Falaschi Cabriolet

Everyone needs advice once in awhile. Delahaye of Paris, France, had been an automaker since 1895 but by 1930, the company was faltering. At a luncheon longtime Delahaye manager Charles Weiffenbach talked to Ettore Bugatti—"La Patron"—about the auto business and asked his advice about the Delahaye car line. Bugatti said they lacked speed and were as heavy as the company's fire trucks.

Soon, Delahayes were put on a crash diet and some redesign took place. In 1933, a new model called the 135 was seen at the Paris Auto Show and earned Delahaye new recognition. Late in 1936, Delahaye added a 4.5-liter (274-cid) V-12 to the car.

Body makers took the Delahaye 135 to stylish levels using art deco curves, swoops and lines. Chapron, Letourner et Marchand and Figoni et Falaschi made Delahayes into works of art.The F and F bodywork was worthy of the Louvre. Designed by Geo Ham, it seemed in full speed even when it was parked.

Chrome sweeps made waves along the rocker panel and covered wheel wells. Side vents on the hood swept back to the body, turning into chrome spears. Tiny jewels of red were inlaid on the tips of the chrome sweeps. A rakishly low windshield was used.

One Figoni et Falaschi Delhaye cabriolet was built for the 1939 New York World's Fair, then was held at U.S. Customs until 1945. After World War II, a filmmaker bought it and inserted a Cadillac V-8. The beautiful car was discovered in 1965 on the property of two elderly women in Fresno, California. Restored in 1973, the car received its original V-12 after the engine was found and retrieved from its storage location in Germany.

The French understand that wine, cheese and art improve with age. And so did the 1939 Delahaye Figoni et Falaschi "California" cabriolet. It is a real example of fine art. Unlike some supercars, no statistics are needed in this case.

Prosper du Bois-Reymond

This exotic Delahaye had only beautiful angles.

Delahaye knew how to make a powerful V-12 engine.

Tom Glatch

1933 Alfa-Romeo 2300 roadster

Alfa-Romeo: **A Reputation Built Through Racing**

From 1910 through 1948, the world's most honored race car was the Alfa-Romeo, winners of 560 races and a company that earned its status through consistent effort as well as style.

The company's roots were in the plant set up in Naples by French automaker Alexandre Darracq in 1906. When it failed, investors named the failed plant Anonima Lombarda Fabbrica Automobil (ALFA). Later, Nicola Romeo bought the business and added his name to the venture. Romeo's charge to designed Vittorio Jano in the early 1920s was to make a Grand Prix race car. That goal led to a string of winners beginning with the P 2 in its first year.

With Italian government backing, Alfa-Romeo offered solid, competitive, sporty cars even through the toughest times of the 1930s. The legendary 1750 went from 0 to 60 mph in just 11 seconds while topping out at 100 mph. The early 1930s produced the 8C 2300 series with its supercharged engine. The unusual dual-geared, split-cam engine reached speeds of 120 mph.

In 1932 and 1933, the 8C finished 1-2-3 in major races like the Mille Miglia and Targa Florio. The smaller Alfas took on Bugattis, Mercedes and Bentleys and often won.

Alfa-Romeo was in and out of racing after the war but continued to build cars with names like the Giulietta, Spyder Veloce, Speciale and Montreal.

To Alfa-Romeo afficionados, their cars are always a short step away from becoming racing tigers. They'll point out how quickly it takes to convert a street version into a racer.

The Alfas carry the heart of a champion and the pride of their nation, built race by race over the years. Alfa-Romeo championship drivers included Tazio Nuvolari, Rene' Dreyfus and Rudolf Caracciola. One other Alfa driver went on to greater things, Enzo Ferrari, who produced a few supercars of his own.

Supercar Classic

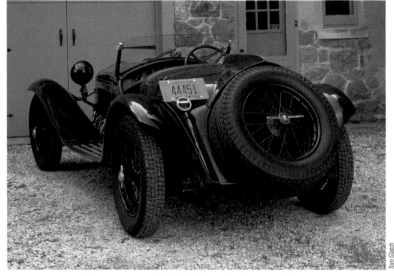

Tom Glatch

From any angle, this Alfa exuded competition.

1947 Alfa-Romeo Convertible

Supercar Classic

Daimler-Chrysler

A classic Maybach phaeton

1921-'40 **Maybach**

Maybach-Motorenbau GmBH is a name that may have been lost to automotive history after 1940 until it was brought back by Daimler-Chrysler Group as a a royal sibling of the Mercedes-Benz. The 2004 Maybach 57 and 62 models carry on the proud tradition of the Maybach family's contributions to the automobile.

Wilhelm Maybach worked closely with Gottlieb Daimler in the 1890s to produce some of the first automobiles. He designed the first Mercedes in 1901. That first Mercedes was considered a major step from the horseless carriage era to reliable automobiles.

Maybach, and his son, Karl, continued in various transportation efforts, especially with their work with the Zeppelin airships. Maybach engines powered those great flying Zeppelins. And the Maybachs also worked on designing and building locomotive engines. During World War II, Maybach engines powered German Tiger and Panther tanks and other military vehicles.

Classic Maybach autos were opulent vehicles and with excellent quality. Among the most famous Maybachs are the 1930 and 1931 Zeppelins— a long, graceful, four-door convertible with artistic speed lines, tasteful use of chrome, flowing fenders and more.

Maybach was famous for its transmission. It featured meshed gears and vacuum assist eliminating the constant use of the clutch in shifting. The classic Maybachs were often compared to the Hispano-Suizas of the period. Manufacured as automobiles of perfection, they are worthy of attention in today's market as are the classic 1921 through 1940 versions.

SUPERCAR STATS	
Engine:	SOHC V-12
Displacement:	7.9 liters (483.4 cid)
Engine Layout:	Front-mounted
Horsepower:	199.9 hp
Top Speed:	170 mph
Weight:	6,173 lbs

KP Archives

1939 Maybach SW 38 four-door convertible

Daimler-Chrysler

2004 Maybach 62 Luxury Sedan

KP Archives

1940 Lincoln Continental convertible

1940-'42 and 1947-'48 **Lincoln Continentals**

After returning from Europe in 1938, Edsel Ford showed Briggs body stylist Bob Gregorie sketches of a car he wanted for family use at Palm Beach, Florida, that spring. It was to be "...fast, active and sporty..." and "...strictly continental..." recalled Gregorie.

The car had a lower silhouette and longer hood than the Lincoln Zephyr it was based on. Edsel insisted on an exterior spare tire in the rear. Popular with the Palm Beach crowd, Edsel told Gregorie it "...leaked like a sieve." Those probems were corrected when production versions debuted in 1939 with other 1940 Lincoln-Zephyrs. At $2,840, it was one of the higher priced cars of the era. The production version had a shorter hood and front fenders than Edsel's car.

The first year, 403 were produced including 54 coupes in their brief May to July production run. In 1941, the Zephyr name was removed and an electric top replaced the vacuum version. Some 1,250 versions were sold including 850 coupes. Just 336 1942 versions with their wide chrome grilles were built, then 1,569 Continentals were sold in 1947 at a stiff $4,500. The restructuring Ford lost $600 per hand-made car and decided to end production after 1948.

Edsel Ford's dream produced 5,324 Lincoln Continentals in all. Said *Motor Trend* in a 1952 retrospective: "...it is [Edsel Ford's] personality that the Continental expresses in its handsome, square lines and that human quality cannot be defined in aesthetic terms. He was a stylist...the Continental is his memorial."

SUPERCAR STATS	
Engine:	Lincoln-Zephyr V-12
Displacement:	292 cid
Engine Layout:	Front-mounted
Horsepower:	120 hp
Bore & Stroke:	2.875 x 3.75 inches
Price:	$2,840

Note: The 1942 and later models had a 305-cid, 130-hp V-12.

1940 Supercars

Angelo Van Bogart

1941 Lincoln Cabriolet

KP Archives

1948 Lincoln Continental convertible

1940-'42 and 1947-'48 Lincoln Continentals |

KP Archives

This 1939 Packard Darrin was owned by Clark Gable.

1939-1942 Packard Darrin Convertible Victoria

1939-1942 **Packard Darrin Convertible Victoria**

One of the most beautiful cars of the pre-World War II era was the customized Packard Darrin Convertible Victoria.

Dutch Darrin, who partnered with Tom Hibbard to form Le Baron in 1921, was a veteran of more than 15 years of coachbuilding when actor Dick Powell asked for a special Packard roadster in 1937. Darrin took a 120 series Packard, shortened the chassis, deleted the rear seat area, and put his trademark "Darrin dip" in the front-hinged doors.

In 1938, Darrin built eight more customized 120 series Packards. They featured rear-hinged doors, less chrome trim and bucket seats. Darrin bought $1,225 Packard business coupes, cut the roofs away, lowered the bodies three inches and inserted new aluminum cowls. Clark Gable bought the first version.

In 1939, ten Packard Darrins were built. They had no running boards, and used rear-hinged doors and bucket seats. In 1940, the Darrin could be ordered from Packard. Experts list one town car, seven convertible sedans and three sport sedans built in 1940 in addition to 30 Victorias. For the 1941 model year, production was switched from the former Auburn-Cord facilities at Connersville, Indiana, to the ex-Sayers and Scoville plant at Cincinnati, Ohio.

The 1941 Darrin had full fender skirts and chrome strips on the fenders and rocker panel. The 1942 version featured horizontal grillework.

Packard's Darrin Convertible Victoria exhibited rarity and style. Introduced in 1940 as the "Glamour Car of the Year." Models 1806, 1906 and 2006 are among the long list of pre-World War II Packard supercars.

SUPERCAR STATS	
Engine:	*Packard 180 series straight-eight*
Displacement:	*356 cid*
Engine Layout:	*Front-mounted*
Horsepower:	*160 hp*
Weight:	*4,121 lbs.*
Price:	*$4,570*

1942 Packard Darrin

1939-1942 Packard Darrin Convertible Victoria

KP Archives

A 1940 (left) and 1941 Packard Darrin (right) in matching red.

Tom Glatch

The 1949 and early 1950 alloy-bodied Jaguar XK-120.

| *1949-1950 Alloy-bodied Jaguar XK-120 roadster*

1949-1950 Alloy-bodied Jaguar XK-120 roadster

During the 1930s, a tradition of style and performance had been developed with the SS 90, SS 100 and the original Jaguar. In 1948, Sir William Lyons wanted a special car to attract attention to his new overhead-cam XK engine at the Earls Court Motor Show that October in London. A roadster, based on the 1938 Jaguar 100 coupe protoype, was developed. Jaguar scarmbled when the XK-120, intended for limited production, became a sensation.

In addition to its low, flowing lines, it was the car's performance that really turned heads. Jaguar chose the 120 name implying that the roadster could go 120 mph but many didn't believe the claim. On May 1949, the XK-120 achieved a 132.6 mph at Jabbeke, Belgium in a speed test. Then Jaguar went racing, finishing first and second at Silverstone in August 1949.

Famed racer Stirling Moss won the 1950 Tourist Trophy in Belfast, Nothern Ireland, racing an XK-120. The Jaguar famed for its license —NUB 120—won three straight Alpine rallies beginning in 1950. It was driven by Ian Appleyard and his wife, Pat, Sir William's daughter.

An XK-120 won a race at Palm Beach, Florida, and a losing driver was so impressed he bought the Jaguar from the racing team—one of the first sold in North America.

The first 240 XK-120s were aluminum-bodied cars. The plan had been to limit production, but the demand forced Jaguar to move to steel bodies in 1950.

In 1951, Jaguar introduced a coupe version that averaged 100.66 mph in a 10,000-mile test. That same year, a beautiful C-Type would begin its string of racing wins. Racing once again proved the mettle of a new generation of Jaguar supercars.

SUPERCAR STATS	
Engine:	DOHC, inline six-cylinder
Displacement:	3442cc (210 cid)
Engine Layout:	Front-mounted
Horsepower:	160 hp
Torque:	195 lbs.-ft. @ 2500 rpm
Price:	$4,745

The interior of the alloy-bodied Jaguar XK-120.

| *1949-1950 Alloy-bodied Jaguar XK-120 roadster*

The long decklid and tail area of the XK-120 Jaguar.

Tom Glatch

KP Archives

1937 Horch Type 930 cabriolet

| *Horch: Forgotten Ring in the Auto Union Logo*

Horch: Forgotten Ring in the Auto Union Logo

In the 21st century, Audi is a well-known carmaker and the brands Auto Union and DKW are memories to those who remember 1950s and '60s imported cars. Yet one of Germany's better pre-World War II automakers, Horch, is simply a forgotten marque.

August Horch was a blacksmith when he began working on engines with Carl Benz in Mannheim, Germany. An innovator, Horch was conscientious about quality and materials. He made aluminum engines and gearboxes, was quick to use a friction clutch and preferred a drive shaft to chain drives—all before Henry Ford's first Model T was produced.

In 1904, Horch set up an operation at Zwickau, in Saxony, Germany. Horch went on to build cars by the Latin version of his name, Audi in 1909. Horch cars continued under a separate ownership and in World War I, the Horch Company concentrated on building armored cars.

The Horch car, roughly comparable to America's Packard of that era, built luxury cars that were sound, reliable and were completed with stately, conservative custom bodies.

In 1932, the Horch car company merged with August Horch's Audi company and they joined with DKW and Wanderer to form the four rings known as the Auto Union.

It was a heady time for Auto Union as many of their cars became legends on the race tracks. The Horch plant built Auto Union racing cars under the guidance of Dr. Ferdinand Porsche.

Horch developed a straight-eight engine in the 1920s, released in 5.0-liter form by 1930. In 1933, the Horch V-8 premiered in 3.0 to 3.8 liter sizes while the 5.0-liter, straight-eight version continued in production.

The Horch cars ended production as the world was thrown into the maelstrom of World War II. Auto Union decided not to continue producing the Horch after the war.

Supercar Classic

1932 Horch Type 670 Glaser-bodied cabriolet

KP Archives

Horch: Forgotten Ring in the Auto Union Logo

KP Archives

1930s Horch Erdmann and Rossi Cabriolet

Doug Mitchel

1952 Maserati A6 GCS Series 1

1952 **Maserati A6GCS Series 1**

A family effort that included five of the six Maserati brothers (Alfieri, Carlo, Ettore and Ernesto from the beginning in 1914 and Bindo beginning in 1932) pooled their talents and experience. The legendary Maserati name cars would soon be seen through a number of classic automobiles. The sixth brother, artist Mario, contributed through his interpretation of the City of Bologna's Neptune logo, now famous as the Maserati symbol.

The successes of Maserati racers helped to secure their place in automotive history, but their road cars also played a role. By the early 1950s, Maseratis were being built by bodymakers like Frua, Pinin Farina and Zagato. They were driven in competition by international racing stars like Stirling Moss of England, Benoit Mussy of France and Juan Fangio of Argentina.

This one-of-a-kind A6GCS Series 1 was built on chassis #2039. It featured bodywork by Guglielmo Carraroli, who was a championship race driver and a talented mechanic. The beautifully curved fenders were easily removed for open-wheel racing events such as Formula II. A 1,978cc, inline-six motor was constructed using a dual-overhead-cam layout developing 130 horsepower at 5,200rpm. Weighing only 1,386 pounds, it was a terrific performer.

This prototype is the only known to exist, but was followed by a Series II edition that was campaigned in 1954. This car was a true Italian supercar beauty.

SUPERCAR STATS	
Engine:	Inline-six, dohc
Displacement:	1978cc (120 cid)
Engine Layout:	Front-mounted
Horsepower:	130 @ 5200rpm
Weight:	1,386 lbs.
Top Speed:	141 mph

Doug Mitchel

This was one of many shapely Maserati cars.

The 1955 Maserati A6 GCS coupe

Doug Mitchel

1953 Cunningham C-3 coupe

1953 Cunningham C-3

Born into a wealthy family, Briggs Cunningham pursued a number of high-level activities before finding motor racing to be his true passion.

Building and racing cars of his own design he found a thrill that was both addictive and productive. Finding himself surrounded by other like-minded fanatics, he created the Automobile Racing Club of America (ARCA) in 1934.

A request from his mother kept him out of the saddle, but his involvement remained high. Following World War II, he found another group of enthusiasts in the SCCA, the Sports Car Club of America, and knew he was "home." His mother's passing allowed him to finally get behind the wheel of his own and others creations.

Even as he campaigned his own team of race cars, Briggs would soon find himself in hot water with the IRS. In an effort to create a legitimate write-off for his racing efforts, the C-3 was built and sold to civilians.

A C-2R chassis of his design was fitted with a Vignale body and an instant classic was born. Only 27 cars were assembled, 18 coupes and 9 convertibles, making them a rare and highly-coveted classic in today's market.

Powered by Chrysler's potent Hemi V-8, it was as powerful as it was beautiful. The combination of limited production, Italian bodywork and Chrysler power resulted in a sticker price nearing $10,000 in 1953. Obviously not meant as your typical family go-getter, the C-3 still sold out quickly, far exceeding Cunningham's abilities to produce cars.

SUPERCAR STATS	
Engine:	Chrysler V-8 Hemi
Coachwork:	Vignale
Chassis:	Cunningham C-2R
MSRP:	$9,000 to $10,000
Production:	27 total (9 convertibles and 18 coupes)

Doug Mitchel

Briggs Cunningham's namesake in coupe form.

Bob Harrington

A 1951 Cunningham C2R on the race track.

Doug Mitchel

1953 Ford Vega

1953 **Ford Vega**

Yes, you read it right, this is a 1953 Ford Vega. Actually, it was a prototype built to gauge potential production, but a Vega nonetheless. Chevrolet's Vega wouldn't hit the sales floors until 1971.

Designed and built for Ford by Vince Gardner, the 1953 Ford Vega took advantage of the inventory found in the Ford/Lincoln parts bins, but turned out an amazing vehicle despite the common gear. Power was drawn from the 60-degree V-8 from Ford that was in its final year of use. Period brochures listed 110 horses on tap from the flathead design. This engine was bolted to a 1939 Ford gearbox that offered three speeds. Added durability was gained by installing gears and axles from the 1939 Lincoln Zephyr.

Holding all this running gear in place was a chassis formed from box-section steel tubing. The design and execution was simple and fairly rigid. A beautifully sculpted body was formed completely from aluminum, saving weight and adding to performance. A set of four elegant wire wheels was finished off with traditional center spinners.

The cockpit was simple with two saddles. Simplicity ruled the roost. A basic instrument cluster hung down from the front cowling as did the upper pivot for the three-speed gearbox. Instead of protruding from the floor, the shift lever sprang from a vertical housing that mounted flush to the firewall.

The shift control fell neatly into the driver's hand. A flat three-spoke steering wheel gave the driver's other hand a spacious place to hold the ample-diameter, period-perfect, skinny, cross-section steering wheel.

This was the only Ford Vega produced. There was nothing common with the later Chevrolet version.

SUPERCAR STATS	
Engine:	Ford flathead V-8
Displacement:	239.4 cid (Nearly 4.0 liters)
Engine Layout:	Front-mounted
Horsepower:	110 hp
Gearbox:	Ford 3-speed, Lincoln-Zephyr gears
Production:	One

Only one edition of the Ford Vega was ever made.

Doug Mitchel

The Ford Vega interior was very simple.

Doug Mitchel

Patrick Paternie

1953 Nash-Healey roadster

1953 Nash-Healey

George Mason, the rotund president of Nash, happened to sail on the Queen Elizabeth at the same time as British carmaker and body specialist Donald Healey. Healey, who had driven for several British carmakers, was working on Healeys using Alvis, Riley and Austin drive trains.

Mason invited Healey to come to the midwest to see the Nash plant at Kenosha, Wisconsin, and to spend some time there. That led to Nash components being sent to Healey's Warwickshire, England facilities. "...he invited me to go fishing with him at his lodge in Northern Michigan," recalled Healey. "In a matter of a few weeks, we worked out the Nash-Healey."

Tests with the Nash engine and drive train in a Healey-Silverstone revealed the Nash underpinnings could become a nice sports car with some better aerodynamics. A new body was created, modeled in part on the 1948 Cisitalia.

The two-seat Nash-Healey roadster had a toothy Nash grille. With the redesign of the Nash lineup, the 1952 Nash-Healey took on an even closer family appearance with pontoon-type fenders fore and aft plus inset headlights. Early in 1953, a coupe was added to the lineup.

The Nash-Healey was entered in the Mille Miglia and Le Mans in 1952 with co-drivers Leslie Johnson and Tommy Wisdom. It placed third at Le Mans behind two Mercedes racers.

The Nash-Healeys used a 252.6 cid ohv straight-six produced 140 hp. The car foreshadowed the Corvette and the Thunderbird and is a supercar worthy of recognition.

SUPERCAR STATS	
Engine:	Nash overhead-valve six
Displacement:	3.8 liters (235-cid)
Engine Layout:	Front-mounted
Horsepower:	127 hp
Price:	$4,063 (1951 only)
	$5,868 to $5,909 (1952-'54)
Weight:	2,600 lbs. (1951 only)
	2,750 lbs. (1952-'54)

A great view of the 1953 Nash-Healey roadster.

The 1953 Nash-Healey also came in a coupe version.

KP Archives

The Gull Wing, doors open, is a classic supercar vision.

1955 Mercedes-Benz 300SL "Gull Wing" coupe

1955 Mercedes-Benz 300SL "Gull Wing" coupe

It was as if a rock and roll band had invaded the dance pavilion and electrified the waltz band. The 300SL "Gull Wing" coupe was to Mercedes-Benz what Little Richard, Fats Domino and Elvis were to 1950s music.

The three-liter Sport Leicht (300SL), like many of the Mercedes-Benz production cars, was a race-inspired car. It began in track form as a Solex-carbureted speedster that won four of the first five races in entered. Well engineered, strong and great looking, it was a natural evolution to bring the 300SL to the public.

The 300SL coupe was the first Mercedes-Benz to use fuel injection, a Bosch unit. What made the 300SL coupe so unique were its doors, a one-piece unit cut into the roof that resembled a seagull's wings when both doors were open.

The racing touch also used a removeable steering wheel and column-mounted four-speed transmission. Topping all that was an extra 40 horses for the fuel injected production version! The 300SL coupe's engine offered 215 hp and a potential top speed of 160 mph. Rock and roll was here to stay!

The best drivers of the era, including Juan Fangio of Argentina and Stirling Moss of England, won major races in the 300SLR.

Mercedes-Benz followed up with the 1957 300SL roadster and 25 more horsepower, up to 240.

You probably won't see one at the 1950s retro cruise. Each version is estimated at $375,000 to $400,000 at auction. Talk about solid gold!

SUPERCAR STATS	
Engine:	Mercedes-Benz
Displacement:	3.0 liters (183 cid), Bosch fuel injection
Engine Layout:	Front mounted
Horsepower:	215 hp
Weight:	2,249 lbs.
Top Speed:	160 mph
Note: "Gull Wing" doors made the car unforgettable	

KP Archives

The Mercedes Gull Wing Coupe was inspired by racing.

1955 Mercedes-Benz 300SL "Gull Wing" coupe

KP Archives

The 1960 300SL Roadster carried on the Gull Wing's success.

Augie Pabst drives the MeisterBrauser Scarab in retro racing.

1957 – 1962 **Scarab Sports Car and F1 racer**

When a wealthy 19-year-old wanted to get into international racing, he jumped in to swim. Lance Reventlow wanted to be better than the competition.

In August 1957, Reventlow Automobiles Inc. (RAI) produced the Scarab sports car in just five months. Designers Dick Troutman and Tom Barnes, drivers Ken Miles and Chuck Daigh, engine builder Leo Goosen, aircraft designer Marshall Whitfield and pinstriping artist Von Dutch contributed to the Scarab.

Just as RAI prepared to compete in Europe, FIA, the Formula One governing body, announced a 3.0-liter engine size limitation. The original Scarabs used a 5.0 liter Corvette V-8. RAI turned with success to SCCA racing. After two seasons, the Scarab sports racers were sold at $17,500 each and work began on the F1.

The F1 used an Offenhauser-based 2,440cc dohc engine with Hilborn fuel injection. The 230-hp engine was tilted at a nearly horizontal angle to keep the hood line low. RAI's facility later housed Carroll Shelby's Cobra productions of the A C Ace and Ford Mustangs.

The Scarabs were crafted at a very high level of excellence, according to one account. In 2004, a rear-engine Scarab F1 was sold at auction for $154,000.

Lance Reventlow died in a plane crash in 1973 but his Scarab lives on in tales of racing and the ranks of supercars.

SUPERCAR STATS

	1957-'58 Scarab sports car	1960 Scarab F1
Engine:	Corvette V-8	Offenhauser-based four
Displacement:	5.0 liter (305 cid)	2441cc (151 cid)
Engine Layout:	Front mounted	Front mounted
Horsepower:	N/a	230 hp
Transmission:	5-speed	Corvette 4-speed
Price:	Inestimable	2005: $550,000 at auction

Note: Sleek molded body. Only three cars built.

1950 Supercars

Doug Mitchel

The Corvette-based V-8 power plant of the early Scarab.

Drivers Augie Pabst (left) and Harry Heuer (right) in a Scarab.

Phil Hall Collection

Tom Glatch

1960 Ferrari California convertible

1958-1963 **Ferrari California Spyder**

What would be finer than a marriage of the exotic, beautiful, racing Ferrari and the sunny, fun-loving state of California in the late 1950s and early 1960s?

The fun-in-the-sun crowd wanted a car that was stylish, fast and helped them with their tans. Their choice was a speedy convertible. And did Ferrari have something special to offer!

Offered beginning in December 1958, the 250 GT California Spyder was a race-bred speedster and needed no makeup or direction for its exterior scenes.

With a 102-inch wheelbase, the Spyder came in both steel and aluminum versions with covered and uncovered headlight lenses. All California Spyders came with knock-off Borrani wheels. Drivers also enjoyed a wooden steering wheel and a ball-shaped shift knob.

In March 1960, Ferrari introduced a 94.5-inch (short wheelbase) version of the California Spyder at the Geneva Auto Salon in Switzerland. This Californian would run and cut as smoothly as a U.S.C. Trojan tailback.

Assembled by Scaglietti of Modena, Italy, 47 long-wheelbase and 57 short versions were on the books, 104 in all, by the end of production in 1963. One of the most famous Ferrari California drivers was actor James Coburn.

Most were powered by the Ferrari 128C engine, a 2,953cc (180-cid) V-12 with aluminum heads and three DCL3 Weber two-barrel carbs.

SUPERCAR STATS	
Engine:	Ferrari 128C V-12, SOHC
Displacement:	2953cc (180 cid)
Engine Layout:	Front mounted
Horsepower:	250 hp
Price:	$13,600
Top Speed:	167 mph
Versions:	94.5-inch, short wheelbase
	102-inch, long wheelbase

1950 Supercars

Tom Glatch

This Ferrari was made for enjoying California sunshine.

Tom Glatch

The California was powered by a 180-cid V-12 engine.

Doug Mitchel

1959 Bocar XP 5

1959 **Bocar XP 5**

The Bocar was built by Bob Carnes of Denver, Colorado. The auto engineer and racing driver felt only he could build the sports car "...for the average guy who wants to race."

Starting with the 88-inch wheelbase X-1 prototype in 1958, the Bocar evolved. The 90-inch XP-5's wheelbase resulted from chrome-moly tubes welded to form a chassis *Motor Trend* claimed was as rigid as a 2-1/2-ton Ford truck. Performance-tuned 370-cid Pontiac or 283-cid Chevrolet V-8s were wedged in place. Bocars also could accept the larger Chrysler V-8.

Lurking under the wheel wells of the 80-pound fiberglass body were 12-inch Buick brakes and twin trailing arms with torsion bars similar to Volkswagens and Porsches. The engine was offset to offer balance with the driver.

Motor Trend writer Len Griffing tested a Bocar XP-5 at Riverside Race Track in California and commented, "On the long straight, it tracks like an arrow and the engine seems to rev without limit. 150 mph came up right now."

The Bocar XP-6 used a 400-hp-plus supercharged Chevy V-8. A sticker price of $11,700 for the XP-6 was $700 higher than the XP-5. Later, the Bocar Stiletto sported a memorable "fish mouth" elongated air intake. Few XP-5s were built and just a handful are still in existence. Only minor victories were added to the Bocar's "win" column.

SUPERCAR STATS	
Engine:	V-8
Displacement:	328 cid (Chevy) or 370 cid (Pontiac)
Engine Layout:	Front mounted
Chassis:	Chrome-moly 41-30 tubes, welded
Body:	Fiberglass molded without doors
Production:	Fewer than 100, all models
Weight:	1,650 lbs. (154-lb. chassis claimed)
0 to 60:	6.0 seconds

Doug Mitchel

Bocars used either Chevrolet or Pontiac engines.

Doug Mitchel

The Bocar interior was very practical but not plush.

1959 Maserati 300S

1959 Maserati 300S

It was probably hard to get a word in with the Maserati brothers, at least about cars. Carlo, Bindo, Alfieri, Ettore and Ernesto entered car racing in 1926. Then their famed brother, Mario, offered his input on the famed Maserati trident logo.

The Maserati brothers soon were known for producing a winner. That success was followed with a car used two coupled V-8 engines to set a world speed record. Wilbur Shaw won the 1939 Indianapolis 500 in a Maserati.

The postwar A6 and 250 Maseratis also were racing winners. Another good racing design came later in the decade in the classic form of the 300S, known for its handling characteristics, acceleration and what drivers considered its feeling of safety. In 1956 competition, the Maserati 300S finished second only to Ferrari in overall points. It continued to be a successful racing car in 1957 with a five-speed transmission in some late versions and larger brakes.

The 300S was considered a reliable car that had plenty of stamina for racing. And its durability held up through the years. By 1984, 19 of the 29 cars produced were still active. One of the more glorious moments for Maserati was in 1957 when Harry Schell and Stirling Moss teamed to pilot a 300S to a second place finish in the 12 Hours of Sebring in Florida.

The 300s had a sleek body built by Medardo Fantuzzi with a low oval-shaped grille. A tubular frame was underneath. On the 1955 cars, air scoops were in the grille, and were moved under the headlights on later models. The 300S ran with triple Weber carburetors. The Maserati 300S used a tubular frame. It had Borrani center-lock, knock off wire wheels.

SUPERCAR STATS	
Engine:	DOHC inline-6
Displacement:	2,991cc (182 cid)
Engine Layout:	Front mounted
Horsepower:	280 hp
Bore and Stroke:	3.4 x 3.6 inches
Top Speed:	180 mph
Weight:	1,720 lbs.

Bob Harrington

The Maserati 300S was a competitive racer.

KP Archives

The beautiful 1971 Maserati Ghibli convertible

Bob Harrington

1952 Jaguar XK-120 coupe

The Racing Jaguars of the 1950s

The Racing Jaguars of the 1950s

On the track, on the oval, over sprint courses, up hillclimbs and through international rallies held throughout the late 1940s and well into the 1950s, Jaguars made their mark.

The success of the XK-120 roadster influenced the C-Type, the winner at the 1951 and 1953 24 Hours of Le Mans. The 2,128 lb. roadster used a tubular frame covered by a sleek aluminum body combined with a 210-hp Jaguar 3.4 liter (207 cid) engine.

While the C-type pressed racing designs, the D-type Jaguar shattered them with its aircraft-inspired styling. The 250-hp D-type engine propelled the car to a 122.39 mph lap record. It won three straight French Grand Prix races from 1955 through 1957.

The D-type was offered only to qualified racers at $10,000 per car and the public clamored for a street version. So Jaguar produced the 1957 XK-SS, the fastest street car produced by Jaguar up to that time. Prospective buyers could get an XK-SS for $6,900, but a fire at the Brown's Lane production facility meant only 16 were ever produced.

Despite the fire, hope remained through the exploits of Brian Lister's 1,904 lb. dark green Lister-Jaguar. It won 11 of 14 races it entered in 1957. And the 1958 version was improved. It produced 300 horsepower and 135 mph.

Racing car developer Frank Costin watched the "Knobbly" Listers and decided to build an even sleeker version for the 1959 racing season. The Costin-Lister used a Jaguar engine with 9:1 compression to produce 250 horses in base form or 300 hp in advanced form.

Mighty Jaguar kept producing fast cats that became supercars through racing. By the end of 1959, the saga was just continuing with the sleeker new E-Type. Its revolutionary design, and those of many more Jaguars that followed, would continue to bring the "cat" supercar status in the decades to come.

1957 Jaguar XK-D

Bob Harrington

1956 Jaguar XK-D

KP Archives

KP Archives

1946 Delahaye 135M Guillere coach

| *Delahaye: The French Beauty by the Fire Truck Maker*

Delahaye: **The French Beauty by the Fire Truck Maker**

Emile Delahaye was a forward thinker. He jumped into carmaking in 1894, admiring the works of Daimler and Benz in Germany. Soon centered in Paris, Delahaye hired Charles Wieffenbach, a man who would leave his imprint on the company from 1898 until its demise in 1953.

Mr. Delahaye was out of the picture by 1901 but the cars that bore his name were just beginning to become popular, in addition to Delahaye trucks, fire trucks and boats.

In 1922, the famed Type 87 arrived in the automotive scene carrying with it the slogan "Sturdy as a Delahaye." Soon, harder times appeared and Weiffenbach needed answers about sluggish car sales.

His friend Ettore Bugatti observed the Delahayes had become too truck-like and lacked speed. Soon the Delahaye cars were changed. The Superluxe premiered at the 1933 Paris Auto Salon and the 135 was introduced in 1934. Both cars began to turned heads on the street and the track and renewed Delahaye sales.

The 135 series provided a platform for bodymakers and accepted an array of engines, including a Delahaye version of the V-12. Delahaye was competitive as well, even winning an event called the Prix du Million (francs, that is or about $80,000). The Delahaye averaged a record 91-mph.

Stylish people wanted to be seen in Delahayes as well. Bodies by Chapron, Guilloie, Letourner et Marchand and Saoutchik were graceful versions of the car. One of the best known versions was the swooping, total-speed look by Figoni et Falaschi.

After World War II, Delahayes attempted to return to their stylish pre-war cars but they developed a reputation for reliability. Also, the French car buyers were looking for smaller, more practical cars. By 1954, they were aborbed by Hotchkiss and *la grand voiture* Delahaye (the great Delahaye car) was gone.

KP Archives

1949 Delahaye Saoutchik cabriolet

| *Delahaye: The French Beauty by the Fire Truck Maker*

1939 Delahaye Figoni et Falaschi-bodied convertible

Doug Mitchell

Supercar Classic

Doug Mitchel

1960 Ferrari T/R 250 Testa Rossa

1960 Ferrari TR/250 Testa Rossa

Enzo Ferrari had built a number of race dominating machines and decided to put an existing 3.0-liter V-12 engine into a sports car chassis. This marriage of engine and coachwork was named the Testa Rossa, Italian for "red head." The name refers to the coloration used on the cylinder heads, and had been applied to other Ferraris in the past.

Chassis number 0666 was the first prototype and was entered in a race at the Nurburgring, located at Eifel, Germany, in May 1957.

Variations were tried as certain forms of bodywork did not meet with Enzo's expectations. Body work for the Testa Rossa was done by Scaglietti and featured a sloping front end with distinctively long front wheel arches. The 1959 TRs were beset with lubrication woes, and subsequent engines were fitted with dry-sump systems.

This 1960 TR/250 featured the latest in dry-sump oiling and had its motor mounted lower in the frame. A four-speed gearbox and rear suspension of either fully independent or De Dion style were fitted. The independent suspension models were referred to as TRI/250.

Production versions featured left-hand steering while the racing versions were available with either left- or right-hand steering.

The 1960 version featured unique and graceful venting on the body sides as well as a tall fin that sloped from the headrest to the tail of the car.

SUPERCAR STATS	
Engine:	V-12
Displacement:	3.0 liter (183 cid)
Engine Layout:	Front mounted
Horsepower:	306 hp
Torque:	281 lbs.-ft. @ 5,500 rpm
Compassion:	9.8:1
Weight:	1,655 lbs.

Doug Mitchel

The Ferrari T/R 250 Testa Rossa used a V-12 engine.

Doug Mitchel

Scoops and arches gave this Ferrari a memorable look.

Doug Mitchel

1969 Maserati Tipo 61 "Birdcage"

1960 Tipo 61 Maserati "Birdcage"

The Maserati Tipo 61 earned its "Birdcage" nickname based on the intricately crafted chassis created with a series of small diameter tubing pieces, welded into a rigid form. Maserati engineer Giulio Alfieri combined the contrary demands of a rigid frame in a lightweight form.

Built to compete in the highly competitive D-modified class, the 3-liter, four-cylinder engine did well. The sensuous body curves, the work of designers Gentillini and Allegretti, both former Maserati employees, belied the ultra-stiff chassis beneath.

This Tipo 61 Maserati example is serial #2455, and was the fourth in the series assembled. Originally sold to Mike Garber for use by racing driver Gaston Andrey, the car saw action in several events. The lightweight, powerful motor and massive brakes delivered a potent punch.

Racing access was to be short-lived. As soon as the front-engined Tipo 61 began to score victories, the format lost favor to rear or mid-engined cars.

One automotive reviewer claimed the Tipo 61 "Birdcage" ran against the grain of the classic Italian sports cars. Even Maserati director Omer Orsi expressed doubts about the Birdcage's frame.

Yet the car grew more famous with time and memories of it. Only 21 copies of the Birdcage were ever assembled, and this is the sole survivor in its original form. The "Birdcage" is a supercar superstar and contributed to a design revolution.

SUPERCAR STATS	
Engine:	Inline-four
Displacement:	3.0 liter (183 cid)
Engine Layout:	Front-mounted, canted 45 degrees
Horsepower:	250 hp
Compression:	9.8:1
Nickname:	Birdcage
Production:	21
Top Speed:	177 mph

Doug Mitchel

A tubular chassis gave the "Birdcage" its name.

KP Archives

A 1948-era Maserati 4 CLT race car.

Bob Harrington

The Chaparral I in its natural setting—on a race track

1961-'62 Chaparral I

By 1960, the team of Dick Troutman and Tom Barnes had earned an impressive reputation for crafting the 1957 and '58 Reventlow Scarabs and for their earlier work with Kurtis Kraft. They had also built their own 1952 Troutman-Barnes Mercury Special.

The T and B team was determined to improve on the progress the Scarab had made in the late 1950s. The result was a Corvette-powered car with a Scarab-like multi-tubular structure, a rear axle with adjustable lateral control arms and a four-speed transmission. Five of the new cars were made, one with an 88-inch wheelbase and four with a 90-inch wheelbase.

Texan engineer and race driver Jim Hall bought the first two "Riverside Sport Racers." Realizing that name wouldn't last, Troutman and Barnes asked him to re-name the car. Hall chose "chaparral," the Spanish name for the roadrunner. That name had a lot of charisma.

Driver Harry Heuer purchased another Chaparral I. Heuer worked for the Peter Hand Brewery and raced his car as the "Meister-Brauser."

"It was the world's fastest skateboard," recalled Heuer in a May 2003 *Road & Track* article. "Driving the Chaparral I was a...combination of feel, sound and fury that was never duplicated by the rear engine cars that followed."

Hall and Heuer raced the Chaparral I with some success, then Hall designed the mid-engine Chaparral II for the 1963 racing season.

Many who remember it say the Chaparral I was the best car of its era.

SUPERCAR STATS	
Engine:	Corvette V-8
Displacement:	5.2 liter (314 cid)
Engine Layout:	Front-mounted
Horsepower:	325 hp
Top Speed:	200 mph+
Weight:	1,479 lbs.
Price:	$16,520

Bob Harrington

The Chaparral I was quite sleek for its time.

The Chaparral I interior, with Corvette shifter, was sparse.

Bob Harrington

1960 Supercars

Doug Mitchel

1962 Maserati 3500 GT Sebring

1962 Maserati 3500 GT Sebring

Named for the fabled race course in Florida, and based on the 3500 FTL, the 3500 GT Sebring delivered American car buyers something they had been lusting for. The Maserati Sebring featured optional air conditioning and an automatic transmission. Neither of these items had ever been available in a Maserati previous to the Sebring.

Beneath the sexy Michelotti-designed and Vignale-crafted shell lurked a 3.5-liter, dual cam six-cylinder engine with 235 horsepower on tap until the larger 3.7 liter V-8 was

installed in the first quarter of 1964. Many drivetrain components were carried over from the 3500 GTI model, including the front disc brakes and all of the suspension. The standard manual transmission was a five-speed ZF model.

Included on the body details was a set of horizontal vents shaved into the lower section of the front quarter panels. These vents functioned as heat extractors on the Sebring Series I cars. Series II models (1965 and later) were seen with high-mounted grilles that provided the same service. The dual headlights and large Maserati Trident in the front grille made for a convincing approach to any gathering.

All of this form and function could run to a top speed in the neighborhood of 135 mph, and reached 60 mph from a standstill in under 8 seconds.

Several hundred Series I cars were sold in its short existence, ranking it high on the all-time Maserati sales charts.

SUPERCAR STATS	
Engine:	DOHC inline-six
Displacement:	3.5 liters (213.5 cid)
Engine Layout:	Front mounted
Horsepower:	235 hp
Top Speed:	135 mph
0 to 60:	Under 8 seconds

Doug Mitchel

The Maserati 3500 GT's body was crafted by Vignale.

Doug Michiel

Inside the Sebring, named for the Florida sports car track.

Doug Mitchel

1964 A. C. Ace

1964 A.C. Ace

With a family tree whose roots reach all the way back to the 1930's, the now fabled A.C. Ace was a sibling to the even more famous Cobra from Carroll Shelby.

Taking an existing A.C. Ace roadster and beefing up the chassis, Shelby had the platform for his next race car. No longer able to drive in competition himself, he retained the desire to build cars for others to run.

Once the chassis was ready a hot Ford 260-cubic inch V-8 was planted between the frame rails. Only the first 75 cars had this motor, while the next 51 received a larger 289. The latter engine produced 271 horsepower in street guise, and could reach 380 horsepower when prepped for racing.

Stuffing all this power into a compact, lightweight vehicle made for some tricky handling, but the overall rush was worth the extra effort. Campaigned on numerous tracks across the U.S., the Ace and later Cobras dominated at events where the mighty Ferrari had once claimed high ground.

1965 would see a crazy-big 427 shoehorned into the Cobra, creating one of the most powerful sports cars ever built.

With a proven blend of power and style, the Cobra has gone on to be one of the most copied cars ever made.

The example seen here is a true 1964 edition of the Ace with a value almost inestimable.

SUPERCAR STATS	
Engine:	Ford V-8
Displacement:	289 cid (nearly 4.8 liters)
Engine Layout:	Front mounted
Horsepower:	271 hp (street version) and 380 (racing)
Weight:	1,685 lbs.
0 to 100:	14 seconds

Doug Mitchel

A Ford V-8 powered the lightweight A. C. Ace.

The 1966 A. C. Cobra 427 roadster

KP Archives

1964 Lamborghini 350 GT

1964 **Lamborghini 350 GT**

Determined he could build a better sports car, Il Cavaliere (the knight), Ferruccio Lamborghini set aside part of the family tractor plant in 1962 to develop a dream car. Giotto Bizzarini, who would later produce his own cars, was directed to make a four-cam racing engine for street use. Engineers Giampaolo Dallara and Paolo Strazani from Maserati and Franco Scaglione joined the efforts to build the car. The dream Lamborghini was to be a "gran turismo" (GT) car that was responsive and yet refined.

Introduced at the 1964 Geneva Motor Show in Switzerland, the 350 GT followed a non-functional GTV version that had premiered at Turin in October 1963.

The Bizzarini V-12 for the Lamborghini was considered state of the art in its day. The engine produced 270 horsepower using the quad cam arrangement. Assembled by Touring at Milan, Italy, the car used independent suspension all around and a five-speed transmission. For years, a rumor has hovered that Lamborghini secretly arranged with Honda to design the Lamborghini engine but the story has never been authenticated.

The beautiful, low coupe had oval headlights that peered above the grille line. Front wheel openings were round while the back pair was squared off.

Lamborghini's dream car was a reality. Way to turn dreams into supercars! Bravissimo, Lamborghini!

SUPERCAR STATS	
Engine:	V-12, quad-cam
Displacement:	3464cc (211.4 cid)
Engine Layout:	Front mounted
Horsepower:	270 hp
Weight:	2,314 lbs.
0 to 100:	17 seconds
0 to 60:	6.8 seconds
Quartermile:	14.9 seconds
Price:	$13,900
Torque:	254 lbs. ft. @ 5,700 rpm

KP Archives

The 350 GT was Lamborghini's debut as a carmaker.

In the 1980s, the Countach was a popular Lamborghini.

Lamborghini Media

John Gunnell

An Excalibur SS phaeton on the road

1965 Excalibur SS

1965 **Excalibur SS**

Designer Brooks Stevens crossed several product lines with his innovative designs in the 20th century touching the lives of many people. In the early 1950s, Stevens designed the slippery-shaped Excalibur J roadster riding a Henry J platform. At least two versions premiered in 1952, one powered by a Willys F-head four and the second used a Henry J L-head six cylinder engine.

A decade later, the floundering Studebaker Corporation needed a car for the upcoming New York Auto Show. Since Studebaker imported Mercedes-Benz cars at the time, Stevens suggested a "Mercebaker," a roadster that resembled the great Mercedes SS of the late 1920s.

Working with a Studebaker-supplied Lark Daytona chassis complete with disc brakes, a Stevens and Associates team crafted the car into the Studebaker SS at the Stevens Milwaukee-area facilities. Young designer Joe Besasie handled many details.

The Studebaker chassis was displayed at the nearby Wisconsin State Fair that year. The Stevens team moved the Studebaker R2 289-cid engine back 29 inches and added a supercharger plus a floor-mounted manual transmission.

While Studebaker was moving to Hamilton, Ontario, the Stevens family displayed the car in New York to great approval. They decided to produce the car beginning in 1965 as the Excalibur SS. It sold for $7,200 and 56 were built. They were 167.5 inches long with a 109-inch wheelbase.

The Excaliburs were supercars that expressed the essence of a dream. The creative minds of Brooks Stevens and Associates made the Excalibur SS and many variants dreams come true.

SUPERCAR STATS	
Engine:	Corvette V-8
Displacement:	327 cid
Engine Layout:	Front mounted
Horsepower:	300 hp
Price:	$7,200
Note: 56 built in 1965.	

John Gunnell

The Excalibur has ties to the famed Mercedes SS series.

1985 Excalibur SS Phaeton, 20th Anniversary

Doug Mitchel

1968 Ferrari 365 GTB/4 Daytona

1968 **Ferrari 365 GTB/4 Daytona**

Replacing the now famous 275 GTB/4 in 1968, the 365 GTB/4 had some big shoes to fill. The 275 had won the hearts of buyers and racers alike, and the flowing, muscular body remains one of the classic designs today.

Unlike many sports and "super cars" through history, the 365 was built using a rear-wheel drive, front engine layout. This conventional configuration lent itself to a road-going touring car, and provided civility for the driver and passengers. Where the 275 had curvy sheet metal, the new 365 featured a chiseled front end. Perhaps in spite of the stark contrast in styling, the Daytona was an instant success for Ferrari. Even outside firms chose this car to clone to offer a lower cost option to those who wanted flash without heritage.

Beneath the long hood was a V-12 engine that displaced 4.4 liters raising horsepower to 352 from the 275's 300. The full-sized body was still capable of being hurled down the quarter mile in only 13.8 seconds in stock form. Terminal velocity was rated at 174 mph. The first U.S.-based cars had uncovered headlights. Later cars all wore the wind-cheating lenses.

In 1969, the drop-top 365 GTS/4 was introduced, and only 127 were produced. Some 1,300 365 GTB/4 models rolled off the line, making them a rare sight. They still are more common than the convertible or "spyder" edition.

SUPERCAR STATS	
Engine:	V-12
Displacement:	4.4 liters (268 cid)
Engine Layout:	Front mounted
Horsepower:	352 hp
Quartermile:	13.8 seconds at 107.5 mph
Top Speed:	174 mph
MSRP:	Just under $20,000 for GTB/4

Doug Mitchel

This Ferrari could reach a top speed of 174 mph.

1968 Ferrari 365 GTB/4 Daytona

The 1965 Ferrari 275 GTB was the Daytona's predecessor.

A 1957 Ferrari 250 T/R in racing action.

The Fabulous Ferrari 250s

Ferrari's great supercar lineage produced the 250 series from 1954 through the 1960s. Ferrari 250 models were stylish, powerful and great performers. In 1954 Ferrari produced the sleek Europa GT coupe with its 180-cid, 240-hp Columbo V-12 engine.

In 1957, a racing terror called the 250 GT Pinin Farina Berlinetta was unleashed and dominated GT racing. Power came from the Tipo 128C version of the Columbo V-12 with its triple Weber carbs. The GT screamed to a top speed of 150 mph and reached 60 mph in just 5.2 seconds.

In 1958, racing regulations spurred Ferrari to look at using the Columbo V-12 in a new car designed for SCCA and CSI World Sportscar racing. It became the famous Testa Rossa. The Sergio Scaglietti beauty was a 1,750-pound car with 300 hp. It won at Buenos Aires, Sebring, Targa Florio and Le Mans.

The 1961 250 GT Berlinetta Competizione used a shortened, lighter wheelbase. Its Tipo 168F Columbo engine used new heads, intake manifold, carburetors and larger valves.

One excellent example was auctioned in California in recent years and $1.45 million didn't budge the reserve.

Giotto Bizzarrini worked on the 1962 250 GT platform and it became a dominant Ferrari race car. When the Ferrari 250 is recalled, many recognize its great bloodline achieved in a decade of competition.

SUPERCAR STATS	
(1962 Ferrari 250 GT coupe)	
Engine:	Twin ohc V-12
Displacement:	2,953 cc (180 cid)
Engine Layout:	Front mounted
Horsepower:	240 hp
0 to 60:	8.8 seconds
0 to 100:	19.8 seconds
Weight:	2,400 lbs.
Top Speed:	134 mph
Price:	$14,367

Bob Harrington

A 1960 Ferrari 250 GT on the race track.

Bob Harrington

A 1964 Ferrari 250 LM takes a turn on the track.

Indianapolis 500 Museum

The 1922 Bentley Indianapolis 500 race car.

Bentley: **Prizes and Prestige**

Bentley has a rich heritage of racing and elegance that qualifies it as a long-term supercar. Walter Owen (W. O.) Bentley was passionate about car racing and produced a Bentley prototype in 1919 as well as a second that raced at Brooklands in 1922. The Bentley 3.0 Liter was put into full production at Cricklewood and was known initially as the TT Replica. Later it was called the Speed Model. A famed Bentley 4.5 Liter called "Old Mother Gun" set a period record of 73.41 mph.

Racers like the "Blower" Bentley inspired production versions that had a strong following. Recently, an unrestored Vanden Plas-bodied 1927 Bentley 4.5 Liter tourer was up for auction at a price of $500,000 to $576,000 U.S.

Bentleys won the Tourist Trophy race on the Isle of Man and the 24 Hours of Le Mans in short order. Bentleys won at Le Mans each year from 1927 through 1930, a feat matched only by Jaguar in the 1950s and nearly 40 years later by Ferrari. Other famous Bentleys have included the 3.5 Liter of 1933 through 1936, the 4.5 Liter of 1936 through '39, the R Type Continental and S Series of the 1950s, the T Series and the contemporary Mulsanne and Turbo R models.

From 1933 on, Bentleys have been built side-by-side with Rolls-Royce. Bentleys always have been considered supercars, on and off the track, with their winged B suggesting racing prizes and automotive prestige.

SUPERCAR STATS (2001 Bentley)	
Engine:	V-8, SOHC
Displacement:	6.75 liter (411.9 cid)
Engine Layout:	Front mounted
Horsepower:	400 hp
0 to 60:	5.96 seconds
0 to 100:	15.5 seconds
Weight:	5,853 lbs
Top Speed:	134 mph
Bore & Stroke:	4.1 x 3.9 inches

KP Archives

1928-'29 Bentley 4-1/2 liter Vanden Plas-bodied Le Mans tourer

Bentley: Prizes and Prestige

Bentley Media

2001 Bentley EXP Speed 8 Le Mans racer

KP Archives

1938 Rolls-Royce Park Ward bodied Sedanca de ville

Rolls-Royce: **The Steinway of the Road**

Henry Royce was so angered by his first car that he decided to build one of his own. Nobleman Charles Rolls wanted to build a car that would be the Steinway of automaking. One Dec. 23, 1904, the two men joined forces and one of the great supercars was born.

Rolls died in an airplane accident in 1910 but Royce lived to see the dream come true. Early on, the rolls-Royce was a great automobile, worthy of supercar status.

From 1907 through 1925, the Rolls-Royce logo was made famous by the silver Ghost series.

Observed the autocar in 1907, "...the motor beneath the bonnet might be a silent sewing machine... there is no realization of driving propulsion...the feeling is one of being wafted through the landscape..."

In trial after trial, the 40 to 50 hp Silver Ghost gained admirers, and that 1907 description carried forward in version after version of the 7,870 produced, including 1,700 made in Springfield, Massachusetts.

Other great Rolls-Royces included the New Phantom (1925-1931), the Phantom II (1929-1935), the 25/30 with its 4,257cc six, the Phantom III (1936-1939), and the short-lived Wraith. Only 491 were produced before the outbreak of war 1939.

After the war, in which Rolls-Royce had gained additional fame as an aircraft engine maker, the Silver Wraith, Silver Dawn and Silver Cloud series cars were produced. And the modern Silver Shadow, the Pininfarina-designed Camargue and other fine cars bearing the "Spirit of Ecstacy" hood ornament and classically shaped radiator have become universal symbols of quality supercars.

Certainly Henry Royce would be proud to drive them and Charles Rolls would agree it was a Steinway of supercars.

KP Archives

1934 Rolls-Royce Phantom II Gurney and Nutting bodied drophead.

1960 Rolls-Royce Convertible

1980 BMW M1 coupe

1980 **BMW M1**

The M1 was BMW's first attempt at producing a mid-engine automobile, and with it they hoped to trounce the dominant Porsche 911.

With no experience of their own in building a mid-engined car, BMW turned to a carmaker that knew those ropes. Chassis design was turned over to Italian carmaker Lamborghini, with its successful history of building mid-body mounted engines. Yet, because of the shakey financial condition of Lamborghini, Baur of Germany also made many of the M1s, according to one source.

For the body, BMW went to another Italian firm and enlisted the talent at Giorgetto Giugiaro's Ital Design of Torino, Italy.

The M1 wore a front grille that sported a modernistic "twin-kidney" opening. The result of this cross-breeding was a graceful yet muscular two-seat coupe. Angular body lines were accented with a set of vertical louvers on the rear quarter panels that helped in cooling.

To power the new car, BMW developed a revised edition of one of their trademark inline-six motors to propel the M1 well over 150 mph..

Displacing 3.5 liters and running dual overhead cams pushing four valves per cylinder, the output was a respectful 277 horsepower. Five speeds were available.

The BMW M1 was only available between 1978 and 1981 when BMW turned its attention to more traditional offerings.

SUPERCAR STATS	
Engine:	Inline-six
Displacement:	3.5 liter (213.5 cid)
Engine Layout:	Mid-body mounted
Horsepower:	277 hp
Transmission:	5-speed
Top Speed:	163 mph
0 to 60:	5.5 seconds

Doug Mitchel

The M1 was the first mid-engined car from BMW.

BMW North America

Artist Andy Warhol painted his version of the BMW M1.

Doug Mitchel

1985 Ferrari Testarossa

1985 Ferrari Testarossa

Replacing Ferrari's aging BB512 in 1984, the latest iteration of the Testarossa brought new levels of luxury and power to the Ferrari owners.

Still motivated by a horizontally-opposed 12-cylinder motor, the package it was wrapped in was the most glamorous ever penned by Pininfarina. The coachwork was low and sleek and was enhanced by horizontal grates on the side panels that led to rear ducts. Within the curvaceous body was one of Ferrari's most luxurious cabins ever.

Acres of soft leather were mated to modern day switch-gear and controls. Directly behind the cockpit sat the powerful 5.0 liter 12. Built with 4 valves per cylinder, the new version of the "red head" motor ("testa rossa" in Italian) claimed 380 horsepower that was tractable and smooth.

A memorable feature of the Testarossa was its side air scoops. The scoops were developed via numerous sesssions of wind testing and were designed to provide ample air for the side-mounted radiators.

To some, they resembled cheese graters and earned that nickname for the prominent air induction openings.

Weighing in at 3,660 pounds, the Testarossa was not the lightest kid in the pool.

Only 5.3 seconds were required to reach 60 miles per hour and a maximum velocity of 178 was there for the taking. It was the perfect weekend getaway vehicle.

SUPERCAR STATS	
Engine:	Ferrari V-12
Displacement:	5.0 liter (305 cid)
Engine Layout:	Horizontally-opposed
Horsepower:	380 hp @ 5,750 rpm
Top Speed:	178 mph
0 to 60:	5.3 seconds

Doug Mitchel

Even the 1985 Ferrari Testarossa engine exuded glamor.

**The fact that all of these Ferraris
are on Goodyear Eagle radials is no coincidence.**

The Formula One Ferrari driven by Michele Alboreto.
Tires: Goodyear racing Eagles.

The new Ferrari Testarossa.
Tires: Goodyear Eagle VR "Gatorback" street radials.

The Formula One Ferrari driven by Stefan Johansson.
Tires: Goodyear racing Eagles.

KP Archives

The 1985 Ferrari Testarossa starred in this Goodyear Tire ad.

Doug Mitchel

1985 Pantera GTS 5

1985 **Pantera GTS 5**

In 1971, you could walk into your local Ford dealer and buy the amazingly cool Pantera from DeTomaso. It was some special kind of Ford!

Power was provided by a Ford 351-cubic inch V-8 mounted amidships in the Pantera. The 310 horsepower was delivered to a five-speed transaxle with 60 mph reached in only 5.4 seconds from a standstill. Even with the bargain price of $10,000 per copy, only 5,600 were purchased between 1971 and 1974, when they were discontinued.

During the 1980s, a few more examples of the Pantera GTS reached the United States. They were built with all manner of bolt-on wings and aerodynamic accoutrements. Performance numbers were boosted, but interest lagged as "real" cars like the Lamborghini offered more bang for the buck.

Taking their wounded pride, DeTomaso gathered cobbled together GTS models and returned fire with the GTS 5 of 1985. The previously rough-hewn body trim was now integrated into the design, resulting in a far more appealing package. The mid-engine design now claimed 350 horsepower from the 5.7 liter Ford V-8.

Flared fenders and a deep front spoiler complemented the huge rear wing.

Not even the slicked-up 1985 GTS 5 could revive sales. The Pantera had seen its best days in the North American marketplace. The Pantera slipped quietly into oblivion.

SUPERCAR STATS	
Engine:	Ford V-8
Displacement:	5.7 liter (348 cid)
Engine Layout:	Mid-body mount
Horsepower:	350 hp
Quartermile:	13.6 seconds at 105 mph
0 to 60:	5.4 seconds

1980 Supercars

Doug Mitchel

De Tomaso brought the 1985 Pantera to North America.

The wing was one of the memorable Pantera body features.

Doug Mitchel

1987 Ferrari 328 GTS

1987 Ferrari 328 GTS

Ferrari's popular line of 308 models received a bump in displacement from 3.0 to 3.2 for 1985 thus replacing the older cars with the latest 328. Sold in both GTB and GTS roof styles, the car delivered more punch in the now classic Ferrari body. Made famous on the TV series, Magnum P.I., the 308 was fairly affordable for those lusting after the graceful lines of the cars.

Carrying a list price of $64,400 in 1986, it made a great "entry-level" purchase for the rabid Ferrari crowd.

The GTS model was fitted with a solid roof panel that could be easily removed and stowed behind the seats until needed. The result was a targa-type open car, the "S" referring to "spyder." The GTB was a true hardtop with a fixed roof with the "B" designation standing for "berlinetta," Ferrari-speak for a coupe.

At least one Ferrari reviewer admired the 328 and called it an inspired new car, not just an evolutionary step from the 308. The 328 proved to be one of the most popular Ferraris ever made.

Under the rear engine cover lurked the improved 3.2 liter V-8 that cranked out 260 horsepower with silky smoothness. The five-speed gearbox provided plenty of options to keep the motor spinning in the sweet spot and could run the quarter mile in just over 14 seconds. 0-60 happened in a respectable 5.6 seconds in capable hands. Front to rear weight distribution was a bit askew at 42/58 requiring a bit of muscle and finesse to get the best results.

SUPERCAR STATS	
Engine:	Ferrari V-8
Displacement:	3.2 liter (195 cid)
Engine Layout:	Mid-body mount
Horsepower:	260 @ 7000rpm
Top Speed:	153 mph
0 to 60:	5.6 seconds

Doug Mitchel

The 328 GTS used a 260-hp V-8.

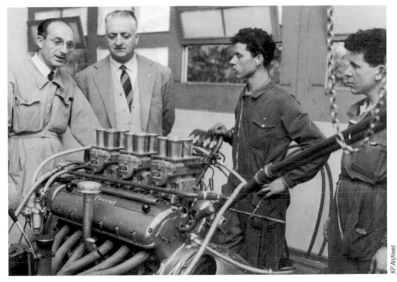

The Ferrari engine was being studied in this period factory photo.

KP Archives

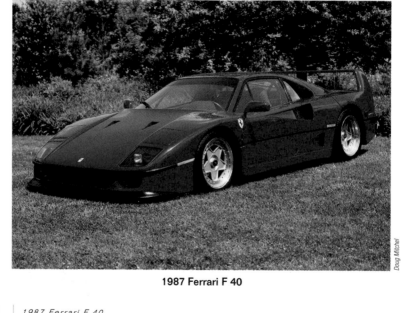

Doug Mitchel

1987 Ferrari F 40

1987 Ferrari F 40

With a track record of building amazing cars for 40 years, a multi-tiered cake would not be enough to mark the pending birthday of Ferrari. Instead, of cake and ice cream, or hats and noisemakers, Ferrari created and released the F40 in July 1987.

Stepping away from the touring machine mold, the Ferrari F40 was close to being a pure race car with license plates.

An ultra-stiff chassis was formed from Kevlar and carbon fiber and the wind-cheating body was mostly a high-tech plastic. The overall contours and high rear wing all added up to a slippery shape that allowed the F40 to reach a top speed of 196 mph. Not bad for a street-legal vehicle of its day!

The V-8 mill measured only 2.9 liters in displacement, but was aided by a pair of turbochargers that brought the horsepower rating up to an astounding 478.

It took a shade less than 4 seconds to reach 60 mph, when the five-speed manual gearbox was stirred properly. An austere cockpit featured seats covered with fire-retarding Nomex, and pull cords to open the doors.

The Ferrari F40 would turn out to be the last Ferrari created under the watchful eyes of the company's founder, Enzo Ferrari.

Ferrari was known as a hands-on type man, always adding input to the design construction of the cars bearing his name. His 1988 caused a near riot in the sales of every just the amazing F40.

SUPERCAR STATS	
Engine:	Ferrari twin-turbo V-8
Displacement:	Mid-body mount
Engine Layout:	Mid-body mount
Horsepower:	478 hp
Top Speed:	196 mph
0 to 60:	3.8 seconds

Doug Mitchel

The F 40 was a race car in street clothing.

The F 40 had a louvered, clear window and a working rear wing.

Doug Mitchel

1982 Lamborghini Countach 4000S

1982–1990 **Lamborghini Countach**

First seen as a show car in 1971, the Countach appeared to be too wild for production, even for Lamborghini. The LP400 featured a 3.9-liter V-12 motor that delivered a 0-60 speed of under 7 seconds. The body was penned by Bertone, and utilized scissor-door mechanisms. An upgraded LP400S debuted in 1978, and added flared fenders, spoilers and crazy-wide tires at both ends.

Tractor-maker/founder Ferrucio Lamborghini, supposedly angered by an Enzo Ferrari comment, decided to build his international-class cars in the mid-1960s. They gained a reputation for their raw speed, good engineering and fine finish. The Countach was conceived by Paolo Stanzani and engineered in part by former Ferrari employee Mauro Forghieri.

Lamborghini released the LP5000S in 1982. The revised car was powered by a 4.8 liter V-12 mill, that remained at 375 hp and could propel the car to 150 mph. The optional rear wing did nothing to enhance performance. The 1988-1/2 Countachs sported fuel injection in North America. Final production of the fabled Countach was in 1990.

SUPERCAR STATS	1985 Countach	1988½ Countach
Engine:	V-12	Quad-ohc V-12
Displacement:	4.8 liter (292 cid)	516 cid
Engine Layout:	Mid-mounted	Mid-mounted
Top Speed:	150 to 173 mph	N/A
Horsepower:	375 to 420 hp	425 hp (U.S.)
Production Years	1974 through 1988	1988 through 1990 (worldwide)
		2005: For auction at up to $550,000

KP Archives

The Lamborghini 4000S body was designed by Bertone.

Lamborghini Media

The 1972 Miura also was a Lamborghini success story.

1987 Porsche 959

1987 Porsche 959

With a well-documented history of building ultra-high performance cars, the release of the 959 was not a complete surprise. The 959 moved the bar a few notches higher and recalibrated the entire thought process. Never a legal vehicle for U.S. use, numerous copies of this truly super car made their way into North America anyway. Porsche would have had to crash test a minimum of four 959s to be considered for legal use in the U.S. and chose not to do so.

Otis Chandler was able to bring one into the country through legal channels for display in his museum located in Oxnard, California. Other examples that may have made it in cannot be driven legally either.

Beneath the gracefully sculpted skins crafted from Kevlar and aluminum, the horizontally-opposed, 24-valve, six-cylinder engine bristled with power and technology. Its 2,849 cc (174 cid) displacement was force-fed by a pair of sequential turbochargers, boosting output to 450 horsepower.

The result of all this technology was staggering. 0 to 60 mph could be reached in only 3.5 seconds and reaching 100 mph only took another 4.8 seconds. A top speed in excess of 198 mph was listed, making the Porsche 959 one of the fastest cars of all time.

SUPERCAR STATS	
Engine:	Horizontally opposed 6-cylinder, turbocharged
Displacement:	2849 cc (174 cid)
Engine Layout:	Rear-mounted
Horsepower:	450 hp
Top Speed:	198mph+
0 to 60:	3.5 seconds
0 to 100:	8.3 seconds
Curb Weight:	2,917 lbs.
Price:	$225,000

Note: 30 959s built to U.S. specs in 1987.

1980 Supercars

Randy Leffingwell

The Porsche 959 was extremely rare in the U.S.

The amazing 959 went from 0 to 100 mph in 4.8 seconds.

Randy Leffingwell

1980 Supercars

1989 Ferrari Mondial T

Kevin May

1989 Ferrari Mondial T

The first Ferrari Mondial coupe was introduced in 1980 and was a true 2 + 2 auto, capable of holding four adults in comfort. Powered by the same 3.0 liter V-8 found in the Ferrari 308 GTB, some 205 horsepower was at the driver's command.

In 1989, the T version of the Mondial debuted, the only version to carry its transmission on a tranverse base. The engine was mounted longitudinally. Only 42 copies of the 1989 Ferrari Mondial T made their way to U.S. shores and this is the only one draped in the striking Prugna paint.

Ferrari Mondial T variants were assembled between 1989 and 1993. The 3.4 liter V-8, taken from the 348, handed out 300 horsepower and could reach a governed speed of 165 mph.

The altered engine layout placed the assembly lower in the chassis, adding to the T's handling characteristics.

Even the bodywork on the Mondial T was modified. Large cheese-grate vents were reduced on the T, but still funneled air into the engine's intake on the driver's side and to an oil cooler on the opposite side.

Enzo Ferrari, whose name is on each of his creations typically played a major role in creating every model built. The Mondial T was one of his last projects to get his studied review before he passed away.

SUPERCAR STATS	
Engine:	V-8 (supercharged)
Displacement:	3.4 liters (207.5 cid)
Engine Layout:	Mid-body mount
Horsepower:	300 hp
Top Speed:	165 mph
0 to 60:	5.5 seconds

Kevin May

The Ferrari Mondial T was a 2 + 2 by design

The Ferrari assembly line, a 1980s sea of red.

BMW North America

1930s BMW 315 Roadster

| *BMW: From Motorcycles to Supercars*

BMW: **From Motorcycles to Supercars**

For the first quarter of the 20th century, BMW or Bayerische Motoren Werke, meant sturdy motorcycles, not cars.

In 1928, BMW bought the floundering Dixi-Werke, an early German automaker, founded by Henrich Ehrhardt in 1896. Dixi was licensed to build British Austin Seven cars. It was called the BMW Dixi at first, then reverted to Dixi.

BMW earned attention with the Austin Seven-based Wartburg Sport, then with the 1173cc 303 series. The 309, 319, 320 and 326 all evolved from it as did the popular 315 roadster.

By the late 1930s, BMW gained attention with the 328 roadster and its 80-hp hemi-head engine that could reach 95 mph in its 1,720 lb. package. The roadster, and a one-off sleek-bodied coupe, dominated 2.0 liter racing in pre-World War II Europe.

In the post-war era, BMW resumed automaking with the 501 sedan, followed by the 502 V-8. By the mid-1950s the large car direction was going nowhere and BMW briefly made the Isetta "bubble car" and the four-passenger 600 version.

The youthful, sporty 507 series coupe and roadster predicted BMW's future. Beginning in 1960, BMW focused a new generation with the 1500, 1800 and 2000 series. Following a merger with Bavarian carmaker Glas in 1966, BMW hit its stride.

By the mid-1970s, BMW was producing the popular 3 and 5 series. The 528 became a popular choice in North America with its 2.7 liter inline six. Later, the elegant 7 series, with its 7.5 liter, 300-hp V-12, was a natural addition. In the late 1990s, BMW introduced its Z series roadsters, worthy competitors to Porsche's Boxter.

Never one to take the short cut or dwell on the quick fix, BMW has always moved forward through racing, solid designs and careful engineering. BMW rose from humble roots to supercar status.

BMW North America

In the 1950s, BMW produced the attractive 507 Series.

KP Archives

The 1983 BMW 320 Cabriolet was popular in North America.

Doug Mitchel

1996 Dodge Viper GTS

1996 Dodge Viper GTS

First seen as a show car in 1989, the Viper RT/10 appeared as an actual production vehicle as the1992 model from Dodge.

With an 8 liter, V-10 motor under the hood, it left no prisoners in its wake. Cranking out 400 horsepower and 450 foot-pounds of torque, the Viper was all at once, king of the performance hill. Never before had a "production" vehicle reached this pinnacle of power wrapped in such a completely bodacious body.

The Viper was intended to be more of a show car that attracted buyers to Dodge dealerships. Its mission was to go from 0 to 100 mph and back to 0 in 15 seconds. And it was a valuable corporate exercise that used new manufacturing and assembly techniques.

In 1996, the hardtop GTS was added to complement the raw beauty of the original Viper. While equipped with even more goodies, the latest adaptation also wore a sleek roofline complete with two aerodynamic "humps." The more powerful 450-horsepower V-10 was beneath the long hood.

The dual side-mount exhaust pipes of the original Viper were supplanted by a full-length exhaust system that terminated under the rear valance. Some suggested that mounting wipers on the side windows might be helpful, especially when the weather turned wet.

SUPERCAR STATS	
Engine:	Dodge V-10
Displacement:	8.0 liter (488 cid)
Engine Layout:	Front-mounted
Horsepower:	450 hp
Quarter mile:	12.8 seconds
0 to 60:	4.4 seconds

1990 Supercars

Doug Mitchel

The hardtop was a 1996 addition to the Viper choices.

Doug Mitchel

The Viper's V-10 engine produced 400 horsepower.

Doug Mitchel

1996 Ferrari 355 Spider

1996 Ferrari 355 Spider

The 355 was first sold in 1995 as a Berlinetta, or hardtop, and was the successor to the 348. Typical of Ferrari nomenclature, the new model featured a mill that displaced 3.5 liters versus the 3.4 of the previous model.

1996 would see the release of the GTS and Spyder versions. The power roof of the Spyder brought all the best features into a single car, and was quickly embraced by current and first-time Ferrari owners.

The 355 would become one of the most successful Ferraris in history with more than 12,000 sold.

The sexy Ferrari coachwork was mated with a sleek convertible top that dropped at the touch of a button. The vented rear deck concealed the potent V-8 motor that pumped out 107 horsepower per liter of displacement.

Gear selection was made with Ferrari's elegant chrome-plated shiftgate and simple shift lever. The mid-engine layout made for nearly perfect weight distribution allowing the driver to put the enormous power to the road effectively and with little fuss. Of course those seeking more excitement could easily flick their 355s into a wicked oversteer condition delighting both passenger and bystander.

Disappearing headlamps were joined by a quadrant of circular tail lamps on the tail-end.

Five-spoke alloy wheels featured the famous Ferrari logo in the center of each, the *Cavallino rampante*. The famous horse design was based on a logo used by Italian national hero and World War I Italian Air Force ace Francesco Baracca.

SUPERCAR STATS	
Engine:	Ferrari V-8, dohc
Displacement:	3.5 liters (214 cid)
Engine Layout:	Mid-body mount
Horsepower:	375 hp
Body Styles:	Spyder, Berlinetta, GTS (Targa)

1990 Supercars

Doug Mitchel

The Spider was a new to the 355 Ferrari series in 1996.

The "cavallini rampale" is a world-famous auto logo.

Doug Mitchel

1998 Lamborghini Diablo VT roadster

Doug Mitchel

1998 Lamborghini Diablo VT roadster

1998 **Lamborghini Diablo VT roadster**

Lamborghini's Countach, innovative when it was first introduced, had grown long in the tooth. Something was needed to rekindle passion and buying demand for the Italian marque. The Diablo (which means "devil" in English) was named for a bull stabled by the Duke of Veragua and the car stormed into the automotive arena in 1990.

Beneath the sleek new Diablo body was a 5.7 liter (349 cid) V-12 engine that produced 492 horsepower at 7,000 rpm. Hoping to enhance performance, or at least to put the current numbers to better use, the Diablo VT debuted in 1993.

The VT (Viscous Traction) system sent power to any of the four wheels on demand allowing far better footing under hard acceleration in slippery conditions. The same 492 horsepower was on tap and 0 to 60 was reachable in 4.5 seconds. Maximum velocity was seen at 202 mph. Adding to the fun of the existing Diablo VT in 1993, the Roadster was introduced. Its removable hardtop could be stowed directly behind the cockpit.

The cabin still was cramped and felt more like a jet-fighter cockpit than a modern sports car.

When the pedal is squeezed, visions of being catapulted off the deck of an aircraft carrier might come to mind. All of this "e-ticket" fun was available at the low price of about $380,000. Get one fast before they're all gone!

SUPERCAR STATS	
Engine:	V-12, DOHC
Displacement:	5.7 liters (349 cid)
Engine Layout:	Mid-mounted
Horsepower:	492 hp
Torque:	479 lbs.-ft.@ 5,600 rpm
0 to 60:	4.5 seconds
Top Speed:	202 mph
Price:	$380,000

Doug Mitchel

The open doors offer a unique look for this Diablo.

Doug Mitchell

The wind-cheating spoiler of the Lamborghini Diablo.

Mercedes-Benz

The 2000 Mercedes-Benz CLK-LM in racing action.

1998-2002 AMG/Mercedes-Benz CLK-GTR series

If you had a bit over $1 million to spend and wanted something special to drive to the local grocery store, the CLK-GTR/SS by AMG/Mercedes-Benz or its racing cousin the CLK-GTR were exciting options for you in the late 1990s and early 2000s.

The Super Sport edition of the CLK-GTR was produced by HWA, a special auto production arm that produces Le Mans-style rare vehicles for the Mercedes-Benz "star" in a racing group known as DTM, or Deutsche Tourenwagen Masters. There also was an LM version of the cars produced for racing.

The AMG/Mercedes was powered by a 7.3 liter (445-cid) V-12 mid-body-mounted engine. This was one mighty Mercedes in coupe form.

Reportedly, the CLK-GTR racer produced 720-hp. There was a smaller, 6.0 liter (365.3 cid), 600 hp version as well.

The CLK-GTR/SS managed the 0 to 60 trip in just 3.4 seconds and the 0 to 100 blur in only 5.7 seconds.

The price of the SS version was $1.25 million in 2002. Owners included a residents of Dubai and Saudi Arabia. If that was too pricey, Mercedes offered the CLK 500 series at about $60,000.

This Mercedes car series was not grand-dad's Studebaker Scotsman!

SUPERCAR STATS	
Engine:	V-12
Displacement:	6.0 liter (366 cid), also 7.3 liter (455 cid)
Engine Layout:	Mid-body mounted
Horsepower:	627 hp
Torque:	516 lbs.-ft. @ 3,700 rpm
0 to 60:	3.4 seconds
0 to 100:	5.7 seconds
Weight:	2,205 lbs.
Top Speed:	191 mph
Price:	$1.25 million

1990 Supercars

Mercedes-Benz

The 2002 CLK 500 was a production version of the race car.

A Mercedes-Benz Formula One car in racing action.

1990 Supercars

Doug Mitchel

1999 Porsche 911 Carrera 4

1999 Porsche 911 Carrera 4

With its niche in the supercar world fairly carved out, the latest iteration of the legendary Porsche 911 was improved at every level.

Long-standing complaints were addressed, and every attempt was made to deliver a truly comfortable car that also hammered out some impressive performance numbers.

In keeping with its heritage, the 911 remained a rear-engine layout but the latest flat six now was liquid cooled and featured dual overhead camshafts. Valve count also increased from two to four on each cylinder. This new recipe fed 296 horsepower to the hungry six-speed transmission. For those seeking a higher level of usability, Porsche's 5-speed Tiptroni S automatic gearbox was available as well.

The new body retained styling cues from previous 911 models but was seated on a three-inch longer wheelbase and was seven inches longer and one inch wider. This sleek wrapping was also fitted with headlights that became part of the sloping fenders, unlike the earlier standup versions. Not only was the latest 911 sold as a coupe, but a soft-top was available.

The cockpit also was turned into a place of great comfort and ease of use. Earlier versions were often viewed as somewhat Spartan and lacking in creature comforts. The latest 911 addressed all of those issues and delivered a cozy, yet purposeful cabin. Leather was everywhere.

SUPERCAR STATS	
Engine:	Porsche horizontally-opposed six
Displacement:	3.4 liters (207.5 cid)
Engine Layout:	Rear-mounted
Horsepower:	296 hp
Transmission:	6-speed manual or 5-speed Tiptronic S automatic
MSRP:	$65,690 (coupe) or $83,820 (convertible)

1990 Supercars

Doug Mitchel

The 1999 Porsche 911 Carrera 4 was improved and upgraded.

A cutaway of the 1999 Porsche 911 Carrera 4

Porsche North America

Jerry Heasley

1969 Corvette ZI-1

Corvette Exotics: **Supercar Versions of the Chevrolet**

The premier of the 1953 Chevrolet Corvette popularized the individualized personal car in the 1950s. Almost from the beginning, Corvette owners made exotic forms of the 'Vettes that could be seen in rallies, drag racing and sports car racing. Many more were customized.

Among the famous Corvette exotics are the cars raced by teams led by Zora Arkus-Duntov. The 1957 Corvette SS ("Super Spyder"), in particular, was a sleek, customized Corvette with a 307-hp V-8 that competed with Ferrari, Mercedes, Jaguar and other cars of the era.

Considered the Holy Grail of the exotic Corvettes is the 1969 ZL1. They came the ultra-rare all-aluminum 427 V-8 that produced 430 horses in production form. It was rumored to run at 585 hp with tuned headers.

In 1996, the Corvette Grand Sport was produced with Admiral Blue paint and a white stripe and two red hashmark accents painted on the left front fender. The 1,000 produced used an LT4 V-8, a 5.7 liter (349.8 cid) engine. This production exotic went from 0 to 60 in 5.2 seconds and had a top speed of 164.9 mph.

Two more exotic Corvettes were produced by Callaway and Lingenfelter. The coach-built 1998 Callaway Corvette C12 used an aggressive, low stance with a Kevlar and carbon fiber body. This $178,500 'Vette used the 5.7-liter ohv Corvette LS1 engine that produced 470 hp and could top out at 188 mph.

The 1998 LPE (Lingenfelter Performance Engineering) Corvette, made in Decatur, Indiana, reached 0 to 60 in just 3.0 seconds with a top speed of 240 mph.

In many eyes, the Corvette already is a supercar. Bring the Corvette up a few exotic notches just solidifies the Corvette in the supercar ranks. And as long as they build them, people will be making exotic versions of the Corvette.

Supercar Classic

Jerry Heasley

1998 Callaway C12 Corvette Speedster

| *Corvette Exotics: Supercar Versions of the Chevrolet*

1998 LPE Twin-Turbo Corvette

Supercar Classic

Doug Mitchel

2000 Ferrari 456 GTA

2000 Ferrari 456 GTA

Ferrari's return to the front-engine and rear-drive platform was achieved with the release of the 456 GT in 1995. Most of the Italian firm's cars had been created in this format but contemporary cars had gotten away from the classic configuration.

The "456" designation also was a break from tradition, as most Ferrari models were badged with numbers that told of their displacement and cylinder count. A 308 was powered by a 3.0-liter V-8—so the identification told a story. The 456 refers to the amount of cc (cubic centimeters) per cylinder in this model but makes no mention of the V-12 power within.

The first 456 GTs were shifted manually with a six-speed gearbox. Even the hard shift gate was in place on this glamorous 2 + 2 model. The GTA added the convenience of an automatic transmission, bringing a new level of comfort to the already well-appointed coupe.

The 456 was built on a tubular steel chassis to which aluminum body panels were bonded with Feran. This provided a complete bond for added stiffness while keeping the assembly light. The 6-speed model weighed in at 3,726 lbs.

The 5.5-liter (335.6 cid), V-12 engine was done in Ferrari style and had all the sounds and power to match.

Inside the cream-colored leather was offset by blue piping as well as matching dashboard and steering wheel. a rather staggering $230,000.

SUPERCAR STATS	
Engine:	V-12, DOHC
Displacement:	6.1 liters (372 cid)
Engine Layout:	Mid-body mount
Horsepower:	442 hp
Torque:	406 lbs.-ft.
0 to 60:	5.0 seconds
Top Speed:	186 mph
Price:	$230,000

2000 Supercars

Doug Mitchel

Ferrari resumed a front-mounted engine with the 456 GTA.

Ferrari used a 5.5 liter V-12 engine in the 456 GTA.

Doug Mitchel

2001 Bentley Azure convertible

2001 **Bentley Azure convertible**

Many of us may desire to own a convertible one day. Thoughts of riding along a winding country road with the top down and feeling the sun on our faces captures much of our free time. Aanother way to look at the convertible option is the Bentley Azure.

Still fully capable of dropping its soft roof and letting the sun flow in, to say the Azure was svelte would be an outright lie. Weighing nearly three tons, it could hardly be considered a lightweight. What it could be considered was one of history's most lavishly-appointed convertibles, or drophead coupes, as the British say.

When folded in its hiding place, the lid closed over the folded top and a super-clean body line remained. It was penned by the legendary Sergio Pininfarina of An enormous 6.8-liter (415 cid), turbocharged V-8 engine was under the "bonnet." The 400-hp, 619 lbs.-ft. mill meant the Azure moved with a 0 to 60 speed of just 6.0 seconds.

A four-speed automatic gearbox shifted seamlessly between the ratios almost mocking the wind as it pushed the Azure at increased speeds. Mileage was only 11 in the city and 16 on the open road.

SUPERCAR STATS	
Engine:	V-8, with Garrett AirResearch turbo and intercooler
Displacement:	6.8 liters (415 cid)
Engine Layout:	Front-mounted
Horsepower:	400 hp
Torque:	479 lbs.-ft.@ 5,600 rpm
0 to 60:	6.0 seconds
Top Speed:	150 mph
Weight:	5,754 lbs.
Price:	$350,000

2000 Supercars

Doug Mitchel

The Bentley's console typified its vast and rich heritage

Doug Mitchel

Bentleys are well-known for their plush interiors.

Doug Mitchel

2001 Ferrari 360 Modena

2001 Ferrari 360 Modena

With its launch at the 1999 Geneva Motor Show, the new 360 Modena from Ferrari was offered as the replacement for the 355.

A first for Ferrari in the GT class was the all-aluminum construction used on the 360. The result of this effort was a car that weighed only 3,064 lbs., yet produced 400 horsepower. This made the 360 131 pounds lighter than its predecessor, the 355, with ad added 25 horsepower on tap.

Obvious in its lack of aerodynamic enhancements, the 360 was fitted with an under-tray that delivered an impressive amount of down force, even at a paltry 70 mph. The sensuous new body work included enclosed headlights in place of the 355's flip-up variants.

Larger front openings drew the oxygen for the powerful engine and rear vents also were added to match the new styling. Measuring 176.3 inches in length and 75.6 inches in width, the 360 was petite. Standing only 47.7 inches tall, headroom was hardly spacious. The cabin was an intimate place to spend some time behind the wheel.

The 90-degree V-8 engine produced 373 lbs.-ft. of torque while spitting out the 400 hp and delivering a solid one-two punch to the competition.

Reaching 60 mph took only 4.5 seconds and a top speed of more than 183 mph was listed. The car's list price was $160,000.

SUPERCAR STATS	
Engine:	Ferrari 90-degree V-8, dohc
Displacement:	3.6 liters (220 cid)
Horsepower:	400 @ 8500 rpm
0 to 60:	4.5 seconds
Top Speed:	"Over 183 mph"
MSRP:	$160,000
Weight:	3,065 lbs.
Note: Five valves per cylinder	

Doug Mitchel

The 2001 Ferrari 360 Modena had an aluminum body.

The Modena is a descendant of the classic Ferrari Testa Rossa.

2001 Mercedes-Benz E 55 AMG

2001 **Mercedes-Benz E55**

Along with their refined, restrained automotive offerings, Mercedes-Benz also sells high performance models. AMG is the in-house division responsible for creating this line, and every example is crafted with running gear and drivetrain. Trim is a set of faux carbon fiber.

The E55 is built on the E Class 500 model. By bumping displacement to 5.5 liters and adding a raft of enhancements, the car created performance that delivered upon request while remaining respectable if asked.

The 0-60 time of 5.4 seconds is reached without any fuss. The motor simply comes to life and responds willingly to any level of input applied. Factory ratings of 349 horsepower and 395 foot-pounds of torque moved the 3,768-pound sedan smartly. (The 2003 version was upgraded to 469 hp.)

AMG, Aufrecht Melcher Grossapach, founded by Hans W. Aufrecht and Erhard Melcher in the town of Grossapach, Germany, produced products for Mercedes-Benz initially, then partnered in auto racing efforts. In 1999, Mercedes-Benz became a majority owner of AMG. The engines now are assembled in Affalterbach, Germany.

"I think this car should have Air Force decals on its flanks starting with the letter F," wrote one reviewer. "The E55 is a speed sled."

While other supercars are able to outperform the E55, very few can do so with four adults and their luggage. Leave it to Mercedes-Benz to make a sedan into a supercar!

SUPERCAR STATS	
Engine:	24-valve V-8
Displacement:	5.5 liters (332 cid)
Horsepower:	349 hp
0 to 60:	5.4 seconds
0 to 100:	12.2 seconds
Top Speed:	155 mph
Mileage:	16 city/23 highway
Estimated Price:	$74,000

Doug Mitchel

A speedy Mercedes-Benz hides in refined sedan trim.

The Mercedes DTM 2000 influenced the E 55 AMG.

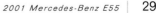

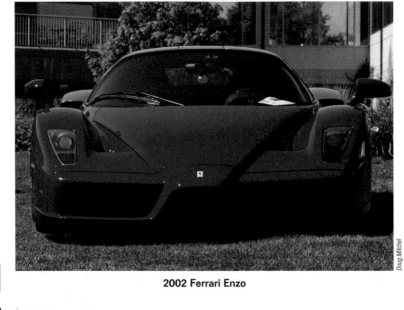

Doug Mitchel

2002 Ferrari Enzo

2002 **Ferrari Enzo**

As soon as it was released in 2002, the Enzo became THE supercar of supercars. It is the ultimate expression of rarity and The 5998cc, V-12 motor uses "Pentroof" combustion chambers to breathe in and out with four valves per cylinder. A quadrant of overhead cams delivers continuously variable timing. A redline of 8,200 rpm requires no less than 95 octane fuel. All of this produces 660 hp at 7800 rpm, with 657 lbs.-ft of torque.

Taking a page from their Formula 1 efforts, the steering wheel holds the shift buttons for the six-speed gearbox. Each gear change can be achieved in 150 milliseconds, providing seamless delivery on the way to the staggering claim of 217.5 mph for this street-legal car.

The curb weight of 3,009 pounds is remarkable, considering the Enzo is not a compact car. Slowing the Enzo from speed are brake pads formed from Carbo-ceramic material, another cue borrowed directly from their F-1 machines. The Enzo's cockpit is one step away from full-race configuration. Primary surfaces are visibly molded in carbon fiber and the seats fit the buyer's physical dimensions. one size does not fit all!

Only 349 copies of the Enzo were produced, with 50 headed to the United States. To see one in person is a rare treat. The MSRP hovered around $750,000.

SUPERCAR STATS	
Engine:	V-12, 65 degree
Displacement:	6.0 liters (366 cid)
Engine Layout:	Mid-body mount
Horsepower:	650 @ 7800rpm
Torque:	485 lbs.-ft. @ 5,500 rpm
0 to 60:	3.65 seconds
Top Speed:	217.5 mph
Weight:	3,230 lbs.
Price:	$750,000

2000 Supercars

Doug Mitchel

The 2002 Ferrari Enzo was inspired by Formula 1 racing.

A smoked-glass cover gave a view of the V-12 engine.

Doug Mitchel

2002 Lotus Esprit

2002 Lotus Esprit

When first sold in the 1970's, the Lotus Esprit, a car that began as a styling exercise, was so well received it was targeted to replace the Europa. The Esprit appeared initially as a concept car at the Turin, Italy, Motorshow in 1972.

Powered by a turbocharged, 4-cylinder motor placed in the middle of the car, the Esprit's rated output was considered to be fairly tame by most standards. Lotus redesigned the sheet metal in 1987, but retained the same four-cylinder power plant.

Model year 1996 saw the installation of Lotus' first-ever V-8 power plant into the Esprit's engine bay. Now rated at 300 horsepower, it was ready to play with the big boys. The 3.5 liter motor was also fitted with a set of turbochargers, helping to boost output from the paltry 140 of its earlier days.

"The Lotus Esprit is...a classic blend with traditional supercar razor sharp edges combined with design elements that have evolved over three decades," commented Lotus Chief of Design Russell Carr.

The fiberglass body's cabin always bordered on claustrophobic, but that mattered little when the car went into tightly wound corners.

Badged as a "Limited Edition" the 2002 wore special trim to mark its passing. A typical model year for the Esprit numbered fewer than 500 cars produced.

SUPERCAR STATS	
Engne:	V-8, twin turbo
Displacement:	3.5 liter (214 cid)
Engine Layout:	Mid-body mount
Horsepower:	350 hp
Torque:	479 lbs.-ft.@ 5,600 rpm
0 to 60:	4.8 seconds
0 to 100:	10.5 seconds
Top Speed:	178

2000 Supercars

Doug Mitchel

The Esprit was originally a Lotus show car.

Every sports car is part Lotus.
And, unfortunately, part something else.

A period ad featured a 2002 Lotus Esprit.

2002 SEMA Pontiac Trans Am convertible

2002 SEMA Pontiac Trans Am

This 2002 Firebird Trans Am was converted to its current status by Custom Design of Trevor, Wisconsin. It was a carefully prepared dream car.

An engineering platform is little else than a unibody lacking any interior or drive train components. This clean-slate starting block offers several advantages to the builder since no existing hardware or paint has to be stripped away before assembly can begin.

Every square inch was coated in the beautiful blue "skin" seen here. Even the underside matches the upper surfaces in luster. Playing a part in the creation of this S.E.M.A. (Specialty Equipment Market Association) vehicle was the historic firm of Hurst, best known for its bulletproof gearboxes. Others were Year-One, Baer and American Racing.

The 3.8 liter V-6 engine is one of four assembled by GM as a potential production unit. Aluminum heads were teamed with an inter-cooled supercharger and a Year-One Ram-Air system. Output is rated at 302 rear-wheel horsepower with 376 lbs.-ft. of torque.

Interior changes included the "Mr. Gasket" logo embroidered into each headrest and Ms. Linda Vaughn's autograph gracing the glove box door.

Additional gauges monitored performance levels.

SUPERCAR STATS	
Engine:	Pontiac V-6, inter-cooled supercharger
Displacement:	3.8 liter (232 cid)
Engine Layout:	Front-mounted
Horsepower:	302 hp
Torque:	376 lbs.-ft. at 2,200 rpm
Quartermile:	Estimated 12.9 seconds
Weight:	2,513 lbs.

Note: Only one example built for 2002 SEMA show.

Doug Mitchel

Many contributors made this special Trans Am possible.

The classic Trans Am coupe was a Pontiac masterpiece.

Pontiac/GM

Doug Mitchel

2002 Porsche Boxter

2002 **Porsche Boxter**

Introduced as an all-new model in 1997, the Boxster was an instant success with the public and media alike.

Daring bodywork wrapped around a cozy cockpit created a stir not seen for many years at your local Porsche dealer. When stowed, the soft top revealed a pair of hoops that protected the driver and occupant in the event of a rollover. A mesh divider helped to keep wind buffeting to a minimum when the top was dropped.

The mid-engine layout delivered a stable, yet very racy feel to the chassis. The Boxster was motivated by a 2.5 liter, flat-six motor and shifted through a five-speed gearbox. For those requiring more power, an "S" model was rolled out for 2000.

The "S" variant Boxster claimed 250 horsepower from its 3.2-liter mill, and featured a six-speed transmission. 17-inch wheels and tires were fitted in place of the 16-inch rims found on the base Boxster. Larger 18-inch wheels could be added as an option.

The 2003 Boxsters were given the gift of more power. The standard model now saw 228 ponies while the S hammered out 258. The new output from the S allowed for 0 to 60 times of less than 6 seconds. I can personally claim a high level of fun is on tap, no matter which blend of Boxster you select. Of course, the Boxster is not a cheap alternative at almost $40,000 per copy.

Adding a few factory baubles can easily get the S model to nearly $66,000.

SUPERCAR STATS	
Engine:	Porsche horizontally-opposed six
Displacement:	2.5 liters (152.5 cid)
Engine Layout:	Mid-body mount
Horsepower:	200 hp
Price:	$39,980

Doug Mitchel

The Boxter was an all-new car from Porsche.

Porsche North America

The Porsche Boxter was introduced in 1997.

Doug Mitchel

2002 Porsche 911 Turbo

2002 Porsche 911 Turbo

Ranking near the top of every automobile enthusiast's list was the time-tested 911. Passing years only bettered the venerable coupe and the 2002 Turbo probably moved up the scale of desirability by several notches in a single step.

One source said that the Porsche 911 Turbo was intended to compete with the Ferrari 360 Modena, the Aston-Martin DB-7 Vantage and the Mercedes-Benz CL-Class.

A 3.6 liter, horizontally-opposed six engine resided beneath the rear deck lid and produced an amazing 415 horsepower in turbo form. The four-second-flat 0 to 60 time was proof of the capability of the puffer 911. One source pegged the car's top speed at 189 mph. For just $18,000 more, you could opt for a factory-installed performance package that added another 35 ponies to the stable.

An almost subtle rear wing kept the 911 Turbo stable at speed and the enormous front grilles drew air to feed the insatiable engine. Having been revamped in 1999, the same smooth body greeted the Turbo, including the flush-mounted headlamps. The cabin also retained its earlier ambiance, making high-speed travel a pleasure.

Standard equipment included power steering, power front seats trimmed in leather, heated outside mirrors, fog lamps, air conditioning and an AM/FM radio.

A convertible version of the 911 Turbo was also offered in 2004. It was the first convertible 911 Turbo offered since 1989.

SUPERCAR STATS	
Engine:	Porsche horizontally-opposed six
Displacement:	3.6 liters (220 cid), turbocharged
Engine Layout:	Rear-mounted
Horsepower:	415 hp
0 to 60:	4.0 seconds
MSRP:	$108,000 (coupe) and $130,000 (convertible)

Doug Mitchel

The Porsche 911 Turbo engine produced up to 415 hp.

2003 Porsche 911 Turbo

Porsche North America

Doug Mitchel

2003 Acura NSX

2003 Acura NSX

Introduced in 1990, the Acura NSX brought supercar performance to the nearly common man. The result of extensive application of aluminum was a curb weight around 300 pounds. Teamed up with a motor that produced 270 horsepower the NSX would prove to be lightning-fast. Along with blinding speed came an ease of use not typically found in high performance cars. Even driven at 8/10s the NSX seemed to be highly capable, even in less than practiced hands.

Cockpits of many supercars are bare boned, leaving luxury trim to other models in the lineup. The NSX also bucked this trend by holding the driver and passenger in a sumptuous interior swathed in leather. Comfortable ergonomics also made the NSX a dream to drive around town at legal speeds.

This combination of comfort and ease of driving was considered to be a hindrance to buyers who sought a more visceral experience when piloting a car of this caliber.

Model year 1995 saw the introduction of the NSX-T that featured a removable hardtop panel allowing open-air driving. This option soon claimed 95 percent of the cars sales, but totals barely reached 1000 for any year. Revisions to the NSX in 2002 saw the hideaway headlights replaced by svelte molded units as well as a few minor tweaks to the contours in the sheet metal.

The 0-60 times were shortened to a speedy 5 seconds, but the latest sticker price of $89,000 for the 2003 models cut deeply in numbers sold. The Acura NSX will be a collectible supercar at some point in the future since Acura decided to end production of the cars.

SUPERCAR STATS	
Engine:	Honda V-6, dohc
Displacement:	3.0 liter (194 cid)
Engine Layout:	Mid-body mount
Horsepower:	270 hp
Top Speed:	165 mph
Weight:	3,000 lbs.

Honda North America

A 270-hp V-6 engine made the slippery NSX a fast car.

The Acura NSX had a leather interior.

Honda North America

Doug Mitchel

2003 Aston-Martin Vanquish S

2003 **Aston Martin Vanquish S**

The Aston Martin badge came to be in 1922 in England and traveled through several variations over the years. The company ended up as Aston Martin-Lagonda, Ltd. in 1958. Ford Motor Company purchased the storied marque during the 1980s and it remains the parent company.

Aston Martin has long been associated with fine, hand-built automobiles and the Vanquish S carried that tradition into this millennium. Modern techology was teamed with old-world craftsmanship and the Vanquish S was testimony to the mating.

Carbon fiber and alloy panels covered the rigid chassis. An aluminum alloy core formed the base and carbon fiber "A" pillars were added. Aluminum double-wishbone suspension was located at all four corners that monitored electronic cornering and traction.

A satin-smooth 6.0-liter (366 cid), 60-degree V-12 engine produced 520 horsepower with PTEC (Power Train Electronic Control) modules that kept everything in synch.

Each Vanquish S was built with the buyer's custom needs in mind and the Vanquish S offered a standard Linn Audio 1200-watt, 12-speaker sound system. The Scottish Linn firm is known for its fine audio systems in private jets and yachts.

From Formula One technology came a pair of paddle shifts on the steering wheel, connected to a six-speed, electro-hydraulic gear selection system.

The Aston Martin Vanquish S price hovered in the $250,000 range.

SUPERCAR STATS	
Engine:	V-12
Displacement:	6.0 liters (366 cid)
Engine Layout:	Front-mounted
Horsepower:	520 hp
Top Speed:	200+ mph
0 to 60:	4.8 seconds
Price:	$250,000

2000 Supercars

Doug Mitchel

The Vanquish S body had a carbon fiber and alloy composition.

Doug Mitchel

The hand-fashioned Vanquish S had modern technology.

The 2003 Porsche Carrera GT was an amazing car.

2003-2004 **Porsche Carrera GT**

Porsche North America summed it up this way:

"It is the sports car our engineers at Weissach were clamoring to build; an unabashed driving machine that serves as a singular expression of speed, power and uncompromising performance."

Now that's an introduction! But, then, the Porsche Carerra GT is some *super* car!

The Carrera GT was the first limited edition Porsche supercar since the fabled 959. One might say the Carrera GT was the new-look Porsche with its all-new styling and its blatant attitude.

New styling was made possible thanks to the Carrera GT's tough but light weight carbon fiber monocoque shell with carbon-fiber reinfored plastic sub frames. The chassis came to Porsche from Italian craftsman ATR.

A mid-body engine mounting was offered to give the Carrera GT a very low center of gravity. A retractable rear wing with its race-like body created a high downforce. Both anti-lock brakes and anti-spin control (ASC) keep the Porsche on the road and on the track.

The Carrera GT's attitude comes from the 349.8-cid water-cooled V-10 that produces 443.5 hp and 435 lbs.-ft. of torque at 5750 rpm. A limited run of 1,500 was expected. The price was $440,000.

It's the sports car many are clamoring to drive!

SUPERCAR STATS	
Engine:	V-10, fuel injected
Displacement:	349.8 cid
Engine Layout:	mid-body mounted
Horsepower:	612 hp
Torque:	435 lbs.-ft.@ 5750 rpm
0 to 60:	3.8 seconds
0 to 100:	6.9 seconds
Top Speed:	205 mph
Weight:	3,190 lbs.
Price:	$440,000 (estimated)

2000 Supercars

Porsche North America

The 2003 Carrera GT seems ready for flight.

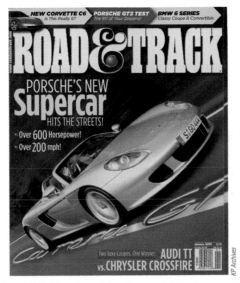

NEW CORVETTE C6
Is This Really It?

PORSCHE GT3 TEST
The 911 of Your Dreams!

BMW 6 SERIES
Classy Coupe & Convertible

ROAD & TRACK

PORSCHE'S NEW
Supercar
HITS THE STREETS!

- Over **600** Horsepower!
- Over **200** mph!

Two Sexy Coupes. One Winner. **AUDI TT**
vs. **CHRYSLER CROSSFIRE**

KP Archives

Road and Track headlined the Carrera GT in January 2004.

BMW North America

2004 BMW Z 4

| *2004 BMW Z 4 3.0i and 2.5i*

2004 **BMW Z 4 3.0i and 2.5i**

In 2004, BMW invited drivers to "Ignite Your Senses" in their beautiful Z 4 roadster, a proud descendent of legendary cars. Available in two versions, the Z 4 came as the 2.5i with a 2.5 liter (152.5 cid) 24-valve dual-overhead cam inline six that produced 185 hp.

Buyers could choose an upgraded 3.0i version with the 3.0 liter (183 cid) 24-valve dual-overhead cam inline six that offered the potential of 225 horsepower and 214 lbs-ft. of torque.

The 2.5i came with a five-speed manual transmission with the SMG (that's Sequential Manual Gearbox) available. Drivers could choose a five-speed, electronically controlled automatic transmission.

The 3.0i came with a standard six-speed transmission or the optional SMG unit with paddle shifters.

BMW puts out some tremendous cars. The Z 4 is in a heritage that includes the 315, 328, 507 and 2000 cars, many of which had racing success.

As BMW promised in its own literature: "Here is a stunning two seater that will ignite your senses every day."

In this case, we can say there is truth in advertising after all!

SUPERCAR STATS	
Engine:	BMW 2.5 or 3.0 liter, both electronic fuel injection
Displacement:	3.0 liter (183 cid) [tested]
Engine Layout:	Front-mounted
Horsepower:	225 hp
Torque:	214 lbs.-ft. @ 3900 rpm
0 to 60:	5.6 seconds
0 to 100:	15.9 seconds
Quartermile:	14.4 seconds @ 95.7 mph
Weight:	3,130 lbs.
Price:	$44,820

BMW North America

The BMW Z 4 seems always ready for action.

The BMW Z 4 competed with Porsche's Boxter.

2000 Supercars

BMW North America

Doug Mitchel

2004 Corvette Z-06 convertible, conversion by AAT

2004 Corvette Z-06 Convertible

The Corvette captured the hearts of the American sports car buyers in the 1950s. By 2001, those who desired more punch could choose the Z-06. With 406 horsepower on tap, and suspension modifications to match, the 2002 and later Z-06 tears the envelope wide open.

Taking a cue from Yenko, Baldwin Motion and Spaulding Dodge of the 1960s, Crossroads Chevrolet contacted General Motors and requested to have two copies of a very special Z-06 built and sold as new Chevrolets. A pair of factory-fresh Z-06s was drop-shipped from the Bowling Green, Kentucky, Corvette plant to the approved shop for alteration. The result is the Z-06 seen here, one of only two built with approval and full factory backing from Chevrolet. It was converted by Advanced Automotive Technologies (AAT) in Rochester Hills, MI, owned by Steve Pasteiner, a GM engineer for nearly three decades.

AAT also produced the 1953/2003 Commemorative Edition Corvettes and the 2000 Buick Blackhawk show car. Once the work was completed, the drop-top Z-06s returned to Crossroads Chevrolet for sale. Carrying the full faith and credit of General Motors, the cars were sold and financed by GMAC. There were far more hopeful buyers than cars available.

Running gear remained unchanged, but the two-tone interior treatment, cross-drilled brake rotors and set of fender stripes were used. No expense was spared in creating the open air versions of the potent Z-06.

SUPERCAR STATS	
Engine:	Corvette LS6 V-8
Displacement:	5.7 liters (345.7 cid)
Engine Layout:	Front-mounted
Horsepower:	406 hp
Torque:	400 lbs.-ft. @ 4,800 rpm
0 to 60:	3.9 seconds
Transmission:	Six-speed manual
Weight:	3,086 lbs.

Doug Mitchel

Only two Corvettes were converted in this manner.

The interior of the Corvette Z-06 was inviting.

Doug Mitchel

2004 Corvette Z-06 Convertible | 333

Cadillac/GM

The XLR was a Cadillac aimed at Mercedes-Benz buyers.

2004 **Cadillac XLR**

Flipping through the pages of automotive history, Cadillac has built more than their share of convertibles. The Titanic-like 1976 Eldorado drop-top was one of the most memorable, if not the largest. The cross-bred Italian Allante was another attempt to bring European luxury to the Cadillac showrooms.

The 2004 XLR was the result of thousands of hours in the R&D labs and was aimed squarely at the Mercedes-Benz SL class buyers. The 4.6-liter (279 cid) Northstar engine pushed 320 horsepower to the rear wheels.

Similar hardware was used on the latest Corvette chassis so the XLR's performance was not to be questioned. A rear-mounted Hydra-Matic 51-50F transmission was integrated with the differential for improved performance in a compact package. The five-speed automatic gearbox delivered nearly seamless transitions between the required ratios.

A four-channel ABS braking system with 12.8-inch front rotors and 12-inch on the rear wheels provided ample stopping power.

Mounted atop all of the mechanical bits was a sharply penned body, complete with a retractable hardtop.

The roof lowered into the rear storage compartment without manual guidance. Dropping the lid cut into the trunk capacity but there was enough room for the luggage needed for a weekend getaway.

SUPERCAR STATS	
Engine:	V-8, DOHC
Displacement:	4.6 liters (279 cid)
Engine Layout:	Front-mounted
Horsepower:	320 hp
Torque:	214 lbs.-ft. @ 3900 rpm
0 to 60:	5.9 seconds
Weight:	3,643 lbs.
Price:	$75,435

2000 Supercars

Cadillac/GM

2004 Cadillac XLR

Cadillac/GM

One look inside lets you know it's a Cadillac.

2004 Ferrari 612 Scaglietti

2004 **Ferrari 612 Scaglietti**

If it resembles a car you may have seen before, the look is intentional. That's because the 2004 Ferrari 612 Scaglietti design is based on a custom-bodied Ferrari 375MM built for actors Roberto Rossellini and Ingrid Bergman in the 1950s. Now that's a pedigree!

The Scaglietti name comes from Sergio Scaglietti, founder of the company that always has done the Ferrari chassis and body assembly. And the same Pininfarina design team that worked on the Ferrari Enzo edition worked on the Scaglietti.

Beautifully crafted aluminum skins cover the body of the Scaglietti. Ferrari claimed the car was both stronger and lighter than the 456 Ferrari series it replaced.

Power for the car comes from a mid-front-mounted 5.7 liter, 540-hp V-8 estimated to propel the 612 Scaglietti from 0 to 60 mph in just four seconds. The engine sits behind the front axle to help balance the car's weight distribution.

Some say Ferrari's goal is to compete with the ultra supercars of the era including the Bentley Continental, various Mercedes models and others.

Inner décor combines leather and aluminum as well as a quality Bose audio system, dual-zone climate control and what an observer called lots of "power goodies."

Sounds like four-place, supercar fun fit for Sergio, Roberto, Ingrid or anyone with enough Euros or dollars left to afford one.

SUPERCAR STATS	
Layout:	Mid-front mounted
Displacement:	6.0 liter (5,748cc) 350.8-cid
Horsepower:	540 hp
Torque:	434 lbs.-ft. @ 5,250 rpm
Bore and stroke:	3.5 x 3.0 inches
Length:	193 inches
0 to 60:	4.1 seconds
Top speed:	195.7 mph
Weight:	4,057 lbs.
Price:	$250,000 (estimated)

2000 SuperCars

Ferrari

The well-sculpted Scaglietti casts a trim profile.

This four-place Ferrari is meant for the road.

Ferrari

Doug Mitchel

2004 Lamborghini Gallardo

2004 **Lamborghini Gallardo**

Being adopted by wealthy parents has its advantages, and after Audi acquired Lamborghini in 1998, new models began to appear.

On the heels of the 2002 Murcielago's success, a smaller, less expensive design was drafted for those wanting Lamborghini supercar fun. Smaller, lighter and far less costly than its bigger sibling, there was still plenty of power and features. Power was derived from an Audi 4.2 liter V-8.

Two cylinders were added and displacement was increased to 4,961cc. The output from the enlarged mill was rated at 500 horsepower and reached a top speed of 192 miles per hour. Some 376 lbs.-ft. of torque reached the driving wheels at 4,500 rpm. Pirelli P Zero tires were mounted on 19 x 8.5-inch front and 29 x 11-inch rear wheels.

A curb weight of 3,100 pounds helped to keep things quick and was 500 pounds fewer than the Murcielago. 60 miles per hour could be reached in only 4.2 seconds.

Permanent all-wheel drive kept the power planted to the blacktop, and a six-speed gearbox offered plenty of choices to the driver.

All of this performance was available for the low price of $160,000, a far more attainable goal for many seeking a high-end Italian vehicle.

Regardless of how affordable the Gallardo is, the angular bodywork gives nothing away and plants the owner firmly in a coveted position of owning a true supercar.

SUPERCAR STATS	
Engine:	V-10, dohc
Displacement:	4.9 liters (303 cid)
Engine Layout:	Mid-body mount
Horsepower:	500 hp
Transmission:	6-speed
0 to 60:	4.2 seconds
0 to 100:	8.2 seconds
Top Speed:	192 mph
Weight:	3,350 lbs.

2000 Supercars

Doug Mitchel

The Gallardo was a smaller, lighter Lamborghini.

Vents kept air flowing to the Gallardo engine and brakes.

Doug Mitchel

Doug Mitchel

2004 Maserati Coupe Cambiocorsa

2004 Maserati Coupe Cambiocorsa

Maserati is another Italian builder with a long, and some say checkered, past. Its history of creating beautiful cars was marred by both quality and management issues.

The return of the American market in 2003 saw several fresh faces marketed and the design and construction was world-class. With Ferrari as their parent company, a higher level of performance and quality became second nature.

In 2003, the 4200GT coupe was introduced and was closely followed by its drop-top cousin, the Spyder. The "4200" designation was dropped but the coupe remains in 2004 and beyond.

A 390-hp, 90-degree V-8 engine is linked to a rear transaxle by a stiff alloy tube that feeds the 390 horsepower to the rear wheels. Displacing 4.2 liters (256 cid) and featuring overhead cams, the output was via a drive by wire throttle with a choice of six gears.

The pretty Coupe Cambiocorsa differentiated from the GT because of its F 1-inspired paddle shift semi-automatic gear selector. All forward gears are shifted using the paddles. The car's cockpit is well-mannered and is equally well-equipped. Leather covers every square inch of the seating as well as much of the other bits and pieces. A 5.8-inch in-dash screen allows control of the audio and internal climate.

The Coupe Cambiocorsa carries the driver and a friend in style and the trunk is designed to carry a set of custom Maserati luggage pieces.

SUPERCAR STATS	
Engine:	V-8
Displacement:	4.2 liters (256 cid)
Engine Layout:	Front-mounted
Horsepower:	390 hp
Top Speed:	177 mph
0 to 60:	4.9 seconds
Weight:	3,682 lbs.
Price:	$85,174

Power was transmitted to a rear-mounted transaxle.

Doug Mitchel

Doug Mitchel

The Coupe Cambiocorsa had a leather interior.

Daimler-Chrysler

2004 Maybach

2004 **Maybach**

Wilhelm Maybach, who had worked for Daimler but parted ways in 1907, and son, Karl, eventually turned their attentions to building beautiful cars with quality automotive engines. The Maybach cars were stunning, solid and used classical styling.

Reincarnating the Maybach name in the 21st century, Daimler-Chrysler set out to build a car that rivaled the Rolls-Royce and Bentley. The "smaller" Maybach 57 is intended to be driver-operated while the 62 is geared towards chauffer driving. The concept of compact does not pertain. The Maybach 57 measures 18.8 feet and the 62 is 20.24 feet. Both cars are 6.5 feet across and 5.15 feet high. The word "prodigious" comes to mind when viewing a Maybach!

Inside is pure luxury, thanks to an enormous catalog of leathers, woods and interior options. A panoramic roof is switched from transparent to opaque at the owner's fingertips. Electronic options included DVD players, 6-CD changers and television sets. Rear seating can be reclined to a nearly horizontal position.

Powering such a large vehicle is no small feat and the Maybach Type 12, twin-turbocharged engine spins out 550 hp at 5250 rpm. A 5-speed gearbox, borrowed from the Mercedes S-Class, is enhanced with a larger torque convertor to manage the new-found power within. Dual "Airmatic" suspension keeps things on the level.

The 57 starts at $310,000 while the 62 begins at $330,000, both higher with numerous options.

SUPERCAR STATS	
Engine:	V-12, twin turbo
Displacement:	5.5 liters (335 cid)
Engine Layout:	Front-mounted
Horsepower:	550 hp
Torque:	663 lbs.-ft. @ up to 3,000 rpm
0 to 60:	57, 5.2 seconds
Weight:	57, 6,050 lbs.
Price:	57, $310,000 +

Daimler-Chrysler

It doesn't get much more luxurious than a Maybach interior.

The double-M is the historic symbol of the Maybach family.

Daimler-Chrysler

Mercedes-Benz

2004 Mercedes-Benz SLR McLaren

2004 **Mercedes-Benz SLR McLaren**

It is part superfast car of the 21st century but it also pays homage to the great Mercedes SLR racers of the 1950s. This remarkable supercar is the product of two great racing names—Mercedes-Benz and McLaren.

The carbon-fiber and composite body and chassis of the coupe has strong influences from the 1950s racers. It is powered by a 5.5 liter (332 cid) V-8 that produces from 617 to 625 hp when pushed and also yields 575.3 lbs.-ft. of torque at up to 5,000 rpm. The new generation SLR breaths thanks to a screw-type compressor that feeds air through "charge-air" coolers and has three valves per cylinder. The SLR also uses a highly refined version of dry sump lubrication.

Mercedes-Benz says each engine is hand-made by a designated Affalterbach engineer who builds it from start to finish. Shifting gears is done with the SLR's five-speed "Speed Shift" unit developed by Mercedes-AMG with manual or automatic modes and in-gear selections that are determined by the driver in manual, comfort or sport settings changed by a dial on the console.

Mercedes-Benz went to the extreme of studying textile weaving techniques to mass-produce its carbon fiber bodies. Another unique feature is an exterior air brake, in this case, a rear-mounted spoiler that can rise to a 65-degree angle when pressure is applied to the brake pedal.

Mercedes-Benz race cars have handed their torch with pride to a new generation of sports cars.

SUPERCAR STATS	
Engine:	Supercharged, intercooled V-8
Displacement:	5.5 liters (332 cid)
Engine Layout:	Front-mounted
Horsepower:	626 hp
Torque:	575.3 lbs-ft. @ up to 5,000 rpm
0 to 60:	3.7 seconds
Top Speed:	200 mph+
Weight:	3,898 lbs.
Price:	$455,000

Mercedes-Benz

The Mercedes-Benz SLR McLaren on fast-forward.

2000 Supercars

2004 Mercedes-Benz SLR McLaren

Mercedes-Benz

The SLR McLaren can cheat any kind of wind.

Mercedes-Benz

2004 Mercedes-Benz SL600 roadster

2004 **Mercedes-Benz SL600 roadster/coupe**

You might think of it as the Teutonic muscle car. This Mercedes is fast enough for any autobahn, yet all the creature comforts are available. It's a macho machine, yet refined as the hand of a princess.

When Mercedes wanted to improve its already terrific SL line of cars in 2004, they took a 493-hp V-12 engine and placed it under the hood of the four-year-old SL500 roadster/coupe. The resulting SL600 is what *European Car* called "…a sterling example of the firm's engineering prowess."

This SL carries on the proud heritage of the venerable 1954 300SL "Gull Wing" Mercedes-Benz, itself a street version of the hot SLR racing car.

Just 500 of the SL600 cars were built, making it even scarcer than the 1,000 SL 55 AMG versions Mercedes produced in 2004.

Since the 12-cylinder engine's clones normally powered the massive Maybach luxury sedans, it had no problem powering the lighter Mercedes-Benz from 0 to 100 mph in less than five seconds.

The SL600 also has a double identity, transforming from roadster to coupe, or vice versa, in just 16 seconds thanks to a hydraulic pump and 11 computer-controlled hydraulic cylinders.

It's one more supercar from Mercedes-Benz. Some day you might be lucky enough to see one—or maybe own one!

SUPERCAR STATS	
Layout:	Front-mounted
Displacement:	6.0 liter 336.4 cid (5,513cc)
Horsepower:	493 hp
Bore and stroke:	3.23 x 3.43 inches
Torque:	590 lbs.-ft at 1,800 to 3,600 rpm
0 to 100 mph:	4.6 seconds
Top speed:	155.3 mph
Weight:	4,299 lbs.
Price:	$125,950
Miscellaneous:	500 made

2000 Supercars

Mercedes-Benz

The SL600 is a rare Mercedes-Benz car.

| *2004 Mercedes-Benz SL 600 roadster/coupe*

Mercedes-Benz

The V-12 engine produces a healthy 493 hp.

Doug Mitchel

2005 Bentley Continental GT

2005 **Bentley Continental GT**

Anyone in the auto market who seeks a big, powerful, well-appointed coupe will more than likely end up at the local Bentley dealer. Once there, the Continental GT will draw attention away from just about any other vehicle on the lot.

With its new parent company, Volkswagen, a ready platform for the GT was borrowed from the flagship VW Phaeton. A two-door body mounted onto a sedan chassis, the GT's dimensions are hardly petite. The liquid lines shaved into the sheetmetal belie its dimensions.

Lift the GT's hood and you are greeted by a massive 6.0-liter (366 cid) engine with a W-12 design. A V-12 engine would have been too long for use in this coupe, or even a large coupe, so the W-12 format was chosen. The GT gets a pair of turbochargers boosting the output to somewhere north of 500 horsepower, with 675 foot-pounds of torque to match.

Hauling a curb weight around doesn't keep the GT from reaching 60 mph in only 4.8 seconds. And 200 mph can also be achieved and exceeded in the GT. Each of the transmission's six forward speeds can be chosen using the paddle-shift mechanism mounted on the steering column. Some have complained about the GT's bulk but naysayers are quickly calmed when pressure is applied to the accelerator.

Part of the GT's appeal stems from its "entry-level" pricing. The entire package of power, luxury and style can be purchased for under $150,000. The first year's production run was sold out before it hit the dealer showrooms.

SUPERCAR STATS	
Engine:	W-12, turbocharged
Displacement:	6.0 liter (366 cid)
Engine Layout:	Front-mounted
Horsepower:	500 + hp
Top Speed:	200+ mph
0 to 60:	4.8 seconds
Price:	Less than $150,000

Doug Mitchel

This sleek Bentley has links to the VW Phaeton.

2000 Supercars

364 | *2005 Bentley Continental GT*

A 6.0-liter W-12 engine lies under this Bentley's hood.

Doug Mitchel

2005 BMW M3 coupe

Doug Mitchel

2005 **BMW M3 Coupe**

The BMW M3 delivers on all fronts as it provides the driving enthusiast with a basket full of styling and performance. Not as luxurious as some, but not as "bare bones" as others, the M3 can handle a day at the track or a day in the country with equal aplomb.

Sold in both coupe and convertible, the M3 draws more true drivers to its hardtop. Differing from the 3-Series platform, the M3 includes flared fenders, an aluminum hood with "power bulge" and M-style alloy wheels in a satin chrome finish. Beneath the bulging hood lies a 3.2-liter, 6-cylinder, DOHC engine that spins out 333 hp at 7900 rpm.

A curb weight of 3,415 pounds requires only 4.9 seconds to reach 60 mph from a standing start. And 155 mph can be reached before the engine's restrictors kick in to limit the pace.

Lurking behind the 18-inch rims under the wheel arches are ventilated disc brakes measuring 12.8 inches on the front wheels and 12.9 inches on the rear wheels. A six-speed manual gearbox provides adequate ratios for any application, short of running in the Daytona 24 Hour event.

The interior is a mixture of Nappa leather seats with inserts of BMW M cloth to hold the occupants firmly in place.

Aluminum trim pieces contrast with the black leather and cloth. A long list of conveniences and safety features make it a great place to spend the weekend!

SUPERCAR STATS	
Engine:	Inline six
Displacement:	3.2 liters (195 cid)
Engine Layout:	Front-mounted
Horsepower:	333 hp
Top Speed:	155 mph (electronically limited)
0 to 60:	4.9 seconds
Weight:	3,415 lbs.
Price:	$47,300

Doug Mitchel

Special styling sets the BMW M3 apart.

Doug Mitchel

A 3.2-liter six powers the 2005 BMW M3.

Doug Mitchel

Cadillac put this version on the race track.

2005 Cadillac CTS-V

2005 **Cadillac CTS-V**

While the angular shape of the Cadillac CTS took some people by surprise, the model turned out to be a success for the well-known marque. Gaining the trust and interest of the younger car buyers was Cadillac's goal, and the CTS proved to do just that. Cadillac also delivered with attention to a racing program.

The standard CTS plays host to a 3.6 liter (217 cid) V-6 engine that provides 255 horsepower. The V gets notched up to a 5.7-liter (348 cid) V-8 mill that hammers out an impressive 400 ponies. The race edition V adds another 100 horses from the 5.7-liter engine.

With each CTS intended for different driving levels, the alterations are understandable. The CTS rows through a five-speed automatic gearbox, while both versions of the V are fitted with a six-speed manual transmission. Suspensions also vary on each version of the cars. The CTS-V racing car rides on a 62.7-inch track as well.

With the more powerful racing engines comes the need for higher-octane fuels. The CTS requires the normal 87 octane while the more powerful V drinks 91 octane. Racing CTS-Vs need 93 octane fuels.

Wheel and tire packages are offered for each on and off track version ot the CTS. The CTS is a new kind of Cadillac, not exactly what some have in mind for the car, but exactly what General Motors was thinking when it created this modern craft.

SUPERCAR STATS	
Engine:	V-8
Displacement:	5.7 liter (348 cid)
Engine Layout:	Front-mounted
Horsepower:	400 hp
	500 hp (race version)
Weight:	3,847 lbs.
	2,900 lbs. (race)
Price:	$49,490

Doug Mitchel

Here's a Cadillac with a youthful image.

2005 Cadillac CTS-V

Cadillac/GM

Doug Mitchel

2005 Chrysler 300C SRT8 logo

2005 Chrysler 300C SRT8

Chrysler introduced the 300 series in 1955, then the most powerful production car available. The 300 later morphed into a succession of letter series cars as the design was altered and upgraded. After a long run, Chrysler returned to its roots with the 300C moniker.

The name is retro but the car is all new. The current iteration features dramatic styling and rear-wheel drive. Several trim levels can meet individual buyer needs and budgetary restrictions.

Another of Chrysler's historic badges was the "Hemi," short for hemispherical heads. The Hemi engine was dominant in the 1950s and 1960s in racing. Cranking out 340 hp, the new Hemi is a force to be reckoned with! When combined with the 300C's muscular body, spacious cabin and luxury appointments, it is an almost perfect combination.

Yet, even coming close to perfection is not enough for some, so the SRT8 version of the 300C was unleashed with a boosted horsepower rating of 425, it now is fortified with a huge dose of power. Front sport seats, additional leather trim and a rear spoiler all make a fast family car even better.

The SRT8's taut body has also been dropped to sit lower in the chassis, augmenting the 20-inch rims at all four corners.

The 300C SRT8 is an affordable bundle of fun! Even fully equipped, the SRT8 delivers all of its power and handling for about $43,000. It certainly offers a lot of bang for the buck!

SUPERCAR STATS	
Engine:	V-8
Displacement:	6.1 liter (372 cid)
Engine Layout:	Front-mounted
Horsepower:	425 hp
Transmission:	5-speed auto with Autostick
0 to 60:	N/A
Weight:	N/A
Price:	$42,995

Doug Mitchel

This square-shaped Chrysler's engine can produce 425 hp.

2005 Chrysler 300C SRT8

Doug Mitchell

This is one Chrysler that was meant for racing.

2005 Ford GT

Doug Mitchel

2005 **Ford GT**

In today's world of supercars, most of the market is dominated by overseas offerings, but Ford's GT now means there is a domestic supercar offering.

In the 1960s, Ford's GT 40, powered by big Ford V-8 engines, earned a reputation for being fast enough to beat Ferrari at its own game. Ford wanted to build a modern, street-legal version that was capable of racing victories and the 2005 GT was born.

Ford engineers set out to build an exotic car for the American public and Ford built a "streetable" car for the masses—or at least 1,500 of the masses.

A rigid aluminum space frame is made from numerous castings and components to form the central tunnel. A 106.7-inch wheelbase carries the 2005 GT with a front/rear weight distribution of 43 and 57 percent, respectively. Overall length is 182.8 inches with a roofline only 44.3 inches from the tarmac.

A 5.4-liter (329.5 cid) V-8 provides power with dual overhead cams and four valves per cylinder. An Eaton screw-type supercharger with intercooler forces in big gulps of air. A sequential, multi-port fuel injection system feeds two injectors per cylinder. The engine produces 550 horsepower.

With an MSRP starting at $143,845, the pain is not as severe as some similar models. Choosing all options bumps the fees to $157,095.

SUPERCAR STATS	
Engine:	V-8, supercharged
Displacement:	5.4 liters (329.5 cid)
Engine Layout:	Mid-mounted
Horsepower:	550 hp
Torque:	500 lbs.-ft. @ 3750 rpm
Price:	$143,845 (base) to $157,095 (with options)

Doug Mitchel

The interior of the Ford GT is simple and straightforward.

Doug Mitchel

The Ford GT name is striped just as it was in the 1960s.

S2000 shown in Spa Yellow Pearl.

Honda North America

The 2001 S2000 fit in well in this desert scenario.

2005 Honda S2000

One might call it the "ultimate Honda" and it certainly is a match with two of the special roadsters from German vehicle makers—the BMW Z 4 and the Porsche Boxter.

The Honda uses a smaller engine than its competitors, a venerable four-cylinder, 2.2-liter (134 cid) power plant that produces 240 horsepower. The 16-valve dual-overhead cam engine features Honda's modern VTEC technology that keeps a greener world in mind as well as speed, power and gas mileage. It means Variable Valve-Timing and Lift Electronic Control.

Produced each year in limited quantities, the S2000 was meant to be an attention-getting sports car that advertised Honda's Formula racing abilities in a street production car. In 2004, it was ranked among *Car & Driver* magazine's "10 Best," an elite category.

With a standard six-speed manual transmission and four-wheel double wishbone suspension, stabilizer bars front and back and gas-pressurized shocks, the Honda S2000 was designed from the ground up as a roadster for track and trail.

The race-inspired Honda S2000 also has a feature that appeared on American cars from the 1930s into the 1950s. It's a push button that fires up the engine.

"The S2000 puts Honda's advanced racing techniques into a car that can be driven every day," say the Honda press people.

One thing they didn't mention is that it's a very affordable member of the supercar ranks.

SUPERCAR STATS	
Engine:	Honda VTEC four-cylinder
Displacement:	2.2 liters (134 cid)
Engine Layout:	Front-mounted
Horsepower:	240 hp
Torque:	162 lbs.-ft. @ 6,500 rpm
Weight:	2,835 lbs.
Price:	$34,000

Honda North America

2004 Honda S2000

A 2001 Honda S2000 shows its appealing profile.

Honda North America

Doug Mitchel

2005 Jaguar XJ Super 8 sedan

2005 Jaguar XJ Super V8

Of all the fine automobiles built by Jaguar, the XJ series is at the top of the scratching post. Of the XJs, the new Super V8 model rules the roost. By taking the long wheelbase (LWB) Vanden Plas and adding more power and accoutrements, the Super V8 was born.

The Vanden Plas edition is not an entry-level Jaguar, but a richly appointed sedan that bristles with the finest materials over every inch of its stretched chassis and perfectly coiffed body. The new Super V8 begins with a more powerful V-8 engine that produces 390 horsepower and includes stump-pulling torque of 399 foot-pounds at 3500 rpm.

A silky-smooth, six-speed gearbox delivers the Super V8 at 60 mph from a standstill in only 5.0 seconds. All of this and the XJ still is capable of carrying four adults in the lap of luxury.

Adding to the impressive array of amenities found in the Vanden Plas, the Super V8 has a DVD touch-screen navigation system installed in the dash. Rear seat passengers can watch movies on the DVD entertainment system with monitors in the headrests.

The latest XJ's stretched wheelbase brings the overall length to 205.3 inches, the longest in its class. Only the Maybach 57 and 62 are longer.

The complete Super V8 has only three options available. Non-standard paint and interior appointments will add $1,000 to the price tag.

A heated windshield costs $300. Adding chrome to the standard 19-inch rims will cost another $2,600. The MSRP for the XJ Super V8 is $86,995.

SUPERCAR STATS	
Engine:	V-8
Displant:	4.2 liters (256 cid)
Engine Layout:	Front-mounted
Horsepower:	390 hp
0 to 60:	5.0 seconds
Weight:	3,810 lbs.
Price:	$86,995

Doug Mitchel

The Super 8 is based on Jaguar's luxury Vanden Plas edition.

| *2005 Jaguar XJ Super V8*

The unique grille and leaping cat proclaim it's a Jaguar.

Doug Mitchel

Doug Mitchel

2005 Lamborghini Murcielago roadster

| *2005 Lamborghini Murcielago roadster*

2005 Lamborghini Murcielago roadster

Joining the Lamborghini family in 2002, the Murcielago (from the Spanish word for bat) fell between the higher priced Diablo and the "entry level" Gallardo models. The roadster appeared in 2004 alongside the coupe and made a nice addition to Lamborghini's offerings. Although carrying a smaller price than the Diablo, the Murcielago has a larger 6.2-liter (378 cid) V-12 engine. It featured 48 valves and a 10.7:1 compression ratio. A massive 575 hp rating is responsible for the 3.7 second 0 to 60 time. A top speed of 200 mph is reachable in the $280,000 coupe. For the thrill of "topless" driving, another $60,000 is required.

A frame crafted from tubular steel alloy and carbon fiber components provides a rigid platform for the remaining suspension and drive train. Front and rear suspension is all of the double-wishbone variety with anti-roll, dive and squat built in for stability and sure-footed handling. Electronic traction control does its job keeping tire slip to a minimum to make the best use of the ponies within. Weight distribution is rated at 42 percent in the front and 58 percent in the rear.

The triangular headrests look right at home in the "bat" as they peek above the low-slung roofline. The seating is designed to be comfortable and is capable of holding the occupants in place. A sound system is included for more than the symphonic sounds emanating from the engine bay.

SUPERCAR STATS	
Engine:	V-12, DOHC
Displacement:	6.2 liters (378 cid)
Engine Layout:	Mid-mounted
Horsepower:	575 hp
Torque:	479.4 lbs.-ft.
0 to 60:	3.7 seconds
Top Speed:	200+ mph
Weight:	3,638 lbs.
Price:	$340,000

2000 Supercars

Named the "bat," this car can fly at nearly 200 mph.

Doug Mitchel

The cockpit of this Lamborghini is all business.

2005 Lamborghini Murcielago roadster |

Doug Mitchel

2005 Lotus Elise

2005 **Lotus Elise**

When handling and performance trump comfort and convenience in your car buying demands, the Lotus Elise will probably be at the top of your shopping list. Capable of amazing performance from a tidy package, the Elise presents an austere cockpit.

The rigid chassis is formed by bonding together aluminum extrusions. The engine sits in front of the rear axle for balance. Displacing only 110 cubic inches, the inline four delivers 190 hp at 7800 rpm. The Elsie is a compact rocket. The 16 valves ride with the aluminum head and fuel injection keeps the cylinders fed with precision. Drivers can reach 141 mph.

The aluminum chassis design creates a pair of flat-bottom tubs that hold the seats in place. The passenger seat is permanently fixed. The driver's bucket can be moved fore and aft. Most of the interior surfaces are aluminum. The stubby gear shift lever is also forged in aluminum and feels like it is directly connected to the gearbox. Short throws provide precise selections and an immediate response.

The illusion of driving a slot car comes to mind when piloting the Elise at any speed above the parking lot velocity. The body is a blend of compound curves and gentle contours offset by rakish air intakes. The rear fascia includes an under-tray diffuser, like those found on modern Formula 1 cars.

All of this fun and more is offered at a fairly low entry fee of $39,000. There are few cars that can provide that much entertainment for the money.

SUPERCAR STATS	
Engine:	Inline-four
Displacement:	1.8 liters (109 cid)
Engine Layout:	Mid-mounted
Horsepower:	190 hp
0 to 60:	4.9 seconds
Top Speed:	141 mph
Weight:	2,000 lbs.
Price:	$39,000

2000 Supercars

Doug Mitchel

Though its a small package, the Elise packs a wallop.

The low, curved lines give the Elise a unique style.

Doug Mitchel

Doug Mitchel

Centered dual exhausts are below the Saleen's rear bumper.

2005 Saleen S281 Mustang

Steve Saleen assembled the first Mustang bearing his name after forming Saleen Autosport in 1984. Along with highly modified Ford Mustangs, he produced the $395,000 S7 in 2003. Powered by a potent 7.0-liter engine that rolled the car to 60 mph in 3.3 seconds, the S7 proved to be a player in the high-end car market. As successful as his S7 model is, the Mustang-based cars continue to be his company's bread and butter .

The S281 seen here is number 81 to be built and is marked as such in the now classic front bumper location. Beneath the hood lies a 4.6-liter V-8 fitted with single overhead cams and three valves per cylinder. The manual version produces 340 horsepower at 4500 rpm with torque numbers to match. S281s fitted with the automatic transmission deliver a healthy 325 hp at 5200 rpm. Spent fumes make a hasty exit through a 2-1/2-inch, free-flow exhaust system.

The Mustang's stock body also is filled with aerodynamic accoutrements to aid in airflow and style. The rear extension allows the taillights to appear set back into the body. A front air dam and additional moldings are placed under the doorsill. Black leather seating surfaces have the Saleen name and logo.

All of this power and beauty doesn't come cheaply, though, with an MSRP of $40,635 for the base S281 and another $2,469 for the larger wheels and tires.

SUPERCAR STATS	
Engine:	Ford SOHC V-8
Displacement:	4.6 liters (280 cid)
Engine Layout:	Front-mounted
Horsepower:	325 hp (automatic) and 340 hp (manual)
Torque:	340 lbs.-ft. @ 4500 rpm
Price:	$40, 635

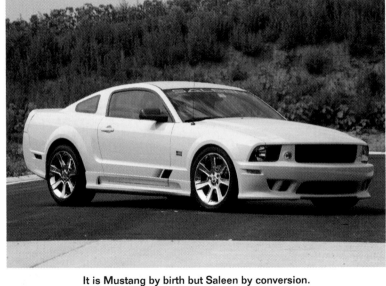

Doug Mitchel

It is Mustang by birth but Saleen by conversion.

2005 Saleen S281 Mustang

The Saleen used Ford's SOHC 4.6 liter V-8.

Doug Mitchel

Jaguar North America

The Jaguar Advanced Lightweight Coupe

Looking for Tomorrow's Supercar

Looking for Tomorrow's Supercar

Will the next supercar be a revolutionary design or will it be a car that is wonderfully retro? Is it possible the next supercar will follow the current direction of hybrids and fuel cell vehicles? Certainly plans are already in the works for the next generation of supercars.

Perhaps the next great supercar will be something like the Jaguar Advanced Lightweight Coupe, a clean-sheet styling example that has been coupled with skilled engineering processes and touched with a dose of Jaguar's racing heritage. The car was designed with a commitment to "...making Jaguars with great design and wonderful interiors, [cars] that are fast, glamorous and evocative."

Another direction for supercars has been demonstrated in Ford's Mustang and the promised Shelby GT 500, Dodge's Charger Hemi, the Chrysler 300 Hemi, and various GM cars and light trucks. They are thoroughly modern, yet styled to make everyone aware of their company's past achievements famous forbearers.

The next generation of supercars could also be the product of new and independent thinking following in the footsteps of today's Kleehans, Koenigsegg and other energetic additions to the automotive world.

With a serious eye on limited fossil-fuel energy resources, the next great supercar may come from the ranks of the alternative energy vehicles like today's Toyota Prius and Honda Insight. Hybrid engines powered in part by batteries or through the sun, hydrogen fuel cells or some new source of energy may lead to supercars of the future.

Whatever shape and direction they take, tomorrow's supercars will continue to build on the advances made in automobiles from the beginning. Supercars always have included generous doses of style, precision, power, engineering and fun.

The supercars of tomorrow will continue to be the superstars of the automotive world.

Hybrids like the Toyota Prius could be tomorrow's supercars.

KP Archives

Looking for Tomorrow's Supercar

A leading "retro" vehicle is the 2005 Mustang convertible.

KP Archives

Looking for Tomorrow's Supercar |

Thanks to the Supercar Owners:

Michael Benet	1989 Ferrari Mondial T
Brian Brunkhorst	1933 Alfa-Romeo 2300 roadster
Robert Colangelo	2004 Lamborghini Gallardo
Cheryl and Michael Flaherty	2002 SEMA Pontiac Trans Am convertible
Joe Hayes	1964 A C Ace
Scott Jerry	2004 Corvette Z-06
Leonard and Leslie Kuznicki	1987 Ferrari 328 GTS
	2003 Acura NSX
Dennis Machul	1933 Alfa-Romeo 8C Monza
	1959 Bocar XP5
Strat Matsas	1996 Dodge Viper GTS
August Pabst III	1928 Bentley 41/2 Liter
Fran Roxas	1939 Cadillac V-16 Opera Coupe
	1953 Ford Vega
John Weinberger	1962 Maserati 3500 GT Sebring

KP Archives

Supercar Owners

Featured Supercars by Tom Collins

Pages 11, 15, 19, 31, 35, 39, 43, 47, 51, 55, 59, 63, 67, 75, 79, 83, 87,
91, 95, 103, 107, 111, 115, 119, 123, 127, 141, 147, 151, 155,
163, 167, 171, 183, 195, 199, 207, 211, 215, 243, 251, 267, 275,
323, 327, 339, 355, 359, 383 and 403.

Featured Supercars by Doug Mitchell

Pages 23, 27, 71, 99, 131, 135, 137, 159, 175, 179, 187, 191, 203,
219, 223, 227, 231, 235, 239, 247, 255, 259, 263, 271, 279, 283,
287, 291, 295, 299, 303, 307, 311, 315, 319, 331, 335, 343, 347,
351, 363, 367, 371, 375, 379, 387, 391, 395, and 399.

Prosper du Bois-Reymond

KP Archives

Supercar Authors

"I hope to achieve perfect silence. The production of these cars will be limited and made with irreproachable care. If I succeed, it will certainly be a vehicle and a piece of machinery beyond criticism."

Ettore Bugatti, April 1931
Writing about his type 41 dream car

KP Archives

Bugatti Type 41 Royale Kellner coach